THE POPPIES CC

CW00833065

THE A TO Z
OF
KETTERING TOWN FOOTBALL CLUB
1979-98

PAUL COOKE

JEMA PUBLICATIONS
1998

Published 1998 by Jema Publications

© Paul Cooke 1998

ISBN 1 871468 83 3

Publisher's Note

Every care has been taken in the preparation of this book and all the information has been carefully checked and is believed to be correct at the time of publication. However, neither the author nor the publisher can accept responsibility for any errors or omissions or for any loss, damage, injury or inconvenience from the use of this book.

Jema Publications
40 Ashley Lane
Moulton
Northampton
NN3 7TJ

Printed and bound in Great Britain by Intype, Wimbledon, London.

ACKNOWLEDGMENTS

To research and write a book such as this has taken a considerable amount of time, I could not have done it without the help of the following people to whom I am deeply indebted.

Without the help and encouragement from Mel Hopkins, for checking my statistics, I would have been slaving away on my computer for an eternity - a big thank you.

To Peter Mallinger, Chairman of Kettering Town Football Club, and Club Secretary Gerry Knowles, for the club's permission to authorise this publication and of cause to all the players and management - without you this would not have been possible,

I would like to thank David Fox, John Harmon, Tim Oglethorpe (of BBC Radio Northampton) and Reg Spiller of the Association of Football Statisticians.

To Tony Noble of Jema Publications who took on the task of publishing this work, his enthusiasm made my final words all the more committed.

One person who deserves a special mention is my long suffering wife Lin, who has endured all my football stories, trivia, and frustrations, not to mention the weekdays and weekends where I disappeared following eleven individuals chasing a spherical object about, without your encouragement and understanding I could not have completed this project.

I would also like to thank Kettering Town's official photographer Mick Cheney, who can be found on the perimeter of the pitch at almost every game with his tackle and finally, the Northamptonshire Evening Telegraph's, Sports editor, Ian Davidson and deputy editor, Derek Waugh, for the use of their photographic and newspaper libraries.

Paul Cooke
Kettering, June 1998

ABBREVIATIONS USED IN THE BOOK

A	Abandoned.
AET	After Extra Time.
APL	Alliance Premier Trophy.
APLC	Alliance Premier League Cup.
APLCS	Alliance Premier League Championship Shield.
BLT	Bob Lord Trophy.
BLTDW	Bob Lord Trophy Drinkwise.
FAC	Football Association Cup.
FAT	Football Association Trophy.
GMACC	General Motors Acceptance Corporation Cup.
GMVC	General Motors Vauxhall Conference.
GOLA	Gola League.
MC	Maunsell Cup.
NSC	Northamptonshire Senior Hillier Cup.
SCC	Spalding Challenge Cup.

* After players name - Loan Players.

Q	Qualifying Round
R	Replay.
QF	Quarter-final.
SF	Semi-final.
F	Final.

This book is dedicated to the memory of Gareth Price, a popular player during the nineties, who sadly died during the final compilation of the book.

REMEMBER THESE HEADLINES?

28 January 1989

FA Challenge Cup
Fourth Round
POPPIES GO OUT FIGHTING
Charlton Athletic 2   Kettering Town 1
Cooke notches another Cup goal in vain

4 January 1992

FA Challenge Cup
Third Round

**DALGLISH TRIBUTE
TO PLUCKY
KETTERING**
Blackburn Rovers 4
Kettering Town 1

'.. I thought Kettering's
players did the club and
their supporters proud.'

**HAT'S OFF TO HELP
BUILD ANEW**

The distinctive 'Tin Hat'
building at the Rockingham
Road end of the ground was
demolished in October 1984.

October 1983

HOFBAUER TO THE RESCUE
Trowbridge 1 Kettering 2

In a season where already Kettering are
finding times difficult. Hofbauer secures
a vital win.

Season 1883/84

**BARNSLEY
CHASE MURPHY**
Second Division Barnsley are
hot on the trail of Kettering
Town striker Frankie
Murphy

FA CHALLENGE TROPHY
4 JANUARY 1992

BLACKBURN ROVERS 4 KETTERING TOWN 1

Phil celebrates his goal in the cup tie against
Blackburn Rovers at Ewood Park

The moment 4,000 Poppies fans at Blackburn will always treasure as
Phil Brown's shot hits the back of Bobby Mimms' net.

FLASHBACK

SEASON 1991-92
BATH CITY 2   KETTERING TOWN 2

A rare sight - skipper Dougie Keast scoring with a header.

SEASON 1994-95
KETTERING TOWN 4   FARNBOROUGH TOWN 1

James Saddington springs up above the Farnborough defence.

INTRODUCTION

Welcome to 'The Poppies Companion - The A to Z of Kettering Town Football Club 1979-98'.

My association with the Poppies began when I moved to the town from the West Midlands during the 1983-84 season and a new found friend, Matt Wilson introduced me to Rockingham Road. My first game though was one I have tried to forget, but you always remember your first game, don't you. Mine was the 0-7 thrashing by Swindon Town in the FA Cup 1st round. After that inept display I wondered what I had let myself in for but the bug surprisingly started there. I kept going back for more until I saw a win, nine games later as it happened.

There have been many crisis periods at the club over the years and during one of those, the 1992-93 season, like so many other passionate fans, I became involved with the fund raising activities to help save the club from extinction. In seasons 1994-95 and 1995-96 I went a step further as the Poppies Programme and Call Line editor.

As an editor articles can take some time to research and write and you need some form of reference book to help you organise your text. Part of this book aims to do just that by featuring every Kettering Town player who has appeared in a first class recognised fixture, even if he has only made a brief appearance during one of the smaller cup competitions. This work is not a comprehensive statistical analysis or historical journal, but every effort has been made to make sure that all records and statistics are as accurate as possible.

With very little, written in recent years about the Poppies, I decided to start with the formation of non-league's Premier Division the, 'Alliance Premier League' which was formed for the onset of the 1979-80 season. Kettering Town have maintained their status in the top flight of non-league football - fraught at times - throughout the Gola and Vauxhall sponsorship and currently, along with Northwich Victoria and Telford United are the only original members left with an unbroken tenure,

As you traverse through this book the following might be helpful to you. A player's appearances include League, FA Cup, FA Trophy, League Cup, Northants Hillier Senior Cup and Maunsell Cup, which are classed as first class fixtures, indeed if the club does not enter the County Cup then it is not entitled to enter the FA Cup. Debuts are a little more complicated. I have included a player's club debut, eg Northants Senior

Cup if it precedes a players Conference debut as some only regard a League, FA Cup & Trophy or League Cup as a true statistic.

Please note that the Daventry Charity Cup, Mitchell & Butlers Cup, and the Midland Floodlit Cup, along with all friendlies have been omitted from this study.

I am sure each one of you has a special memory of some of the players featured in this work, and while I impress mine, this may not be the definitive article.

This book should have originally been on the market for Christmas 1997, but with the Poppies propping up the Conference and possible relegation, GM Vauxhall's decision to terminate their sponsorship of the Conference, a proposed merger and ground development with Corby Town at Rockingham Triangle, a possible fans buy out if the Corby solution went ahead, a new ground site option at Cohen's Yard, another seasons worth of players and statistics, plus (thankfully), a turn around in fortunes and results, I decided to wait until the, end of the 1997-98 season before going ahead - hopefully with all the above issues mere history.

I would like to part dedicate this work, one I have thoroughly enjoyed researching, to the Kettering Town fans, who simply are the best, you have been tremendous throughout the first 19 seasons of competitive play. Smaller clubs rely on their loyal supporters and the Poppies fans have done their club proud. There are many memorable moments - the dizzy FA Cup runs, the barmy away days, the throwing of the league away in the final few matches of the season scenario, the Dunkirk spirit when the club is going through one of its crisis, etc, etc - but at the end of the day the true Poppies fan is still there cheering on the team in hope of that illustrious dream - promotion to the Football League.

Paul Cooke
June 1998
Kettering,.

A

ADAMS CARL. Midfield. Previous club: Stevenage Borough. A Steve Berry capture during the 1997-98 close season. Scored his first goal for the club in the 4-2 away win against Cambridge City in the FA Cup 2nd Qualifying round replay - Kettering won 4-2 after extra time. Scored his first Conference goals, (a brace, one a penalty), against Morecambe in Kettering's 3-1 away win - their first against the Shrimpers, since their elevation to non-league's top flight.

GM Vauxhall Conference, debut v Woking (h) 09:09:97

Appearances: 39　　League 31　　**Goals:** 7　　League 5
　　　　　　　　　　　Cups　8　　　　　　　　　　　Cups　2

ADAMS STEVE. Winger. Born Sheffield. Previous clubs: Rotherham United, Worksop Town, Scarborough, Doncaster Rovers, Manawater United (New Zealand) and Boston United. Steve was signed during the summer of 1992 by Dave Cusack after a spell coaching in the USA but was soon released once Graham Carr took over. Later played for Macclesfield Town.

Debut (Maunsell Cup) v Peterborough United (h) 08:08:92
GM Vauxhall Conference, debut v Slough Town (a) 22:08:92.

Appearances: 13　　League 9+2　　**Goals:** 0
　　　　　　　　　　　Cups 2

ALEXANDER KEITH. Forward. Born Nottingham. Previous clubs: Kings Lynn, Boston United, Spalding, Grantham and Stamford. While at Stamford he played in the 1980 FA Vase Final at Wembley. Keith joined the Poppies from Kings Lynn during the 1984-85 pre-season, and left disappointingly to join Barnet at the start of the 1986-87 season. Although never a prolific goalscorer, he chipped in with a few. Keith scored his first goal for the club in the 1-2 home defeat by Bath City on September 1st 1984.

Debut (Maunsell Cup) v Peterborough United (h) 15:08:84
Gola League, debut v Altrincham (a) 18:08:84

Appearances: 74   League 46+13   **Goals:** 11   League 8
Cups   12+2   Cups   3

ALFORD CARL. Striker. Born Manchester. Carl became quite a sensation, a prolific centre-forward who had one of the best goal ratios per number of games played during his career with the Poppies. He was signed from Macclesfield Town for a club record fee of £25,000 during the 1994-95 close season, scoring 27 goals in his first season including a hat-trick against Bromsgrove Rovers on the final day of the 1994-95 campaign. In his second season he netted 27 goals again scoring a hat-trick, this time against Altrincham - making the Robins his favourite side to score against with 8 goals in 4 matches. In February 1996 he was selected to play for the England semi-professional side against the Republic of Ireland at Kidderminster Harriers - true to form he became the first Poppies' player to score for the National side. In March 1996 he was sold to neighbours Rushden & Diamonds for £85,000 (a record between two non-league clubs) on transfer deadline day. Carl also played for Burnley, Stockport County, Morecambe (loan), Rochdale and Witton Albion - where he played in the 1991-92 FA Trophy Final at Wembley against Colchester United. During his successful time at Nene Park Carl was under much speculation of returning to Rockingham Road, before playing for Dover Athletic and finally ending rumours by signing for Stevenage Borough for the onset of the 1998-99 campaign.

GM Vauxhall Conference, debut v Runcorn (a) 20:08:94

Appearances: 94   League 67+2   **Goals:** 54   League 45
Cups   24+1   Cups   9

ALLIANCE PREMIER LEAGUE. Formed for the on set of the 1979-80 season. Non-league's Premier Division was comprised of 20 teams, 13 from the Southern League and 7 from the Northern League. Even though this division gave non-league a professional standing, promotion to Division 4 was not automatic, it still relied on the ballot box, as Altrincham were to find out as the first winners of the Alliance, failing to gain promotion by one vote. The Poppies finished in 7th place. The Alliance Premier League kept its title until the end of the 1983-84 season, when it was succeeded by the Gola League.

Carl Alford - dynamic Striker

ALLIANCE PREMIER LEAGUE CUP. The competition for the first four seasons was in fact the Bob Lord Trophy (as it was later known). The trophy, a cup which has been used in various guises over the 19 seasons, is made from solid silver and stands 20" or 508mm high. It was made in 1933 and is London Hall-Marked. At the beginning of World War Two the cup was placed in a strong room and was lost for many years until 1979. Named after Mr Bob Lord, the first president of the Alliance Premier League. He was a great believer in football's premier non-league clubs having the chance to join the Football League. The Poppies most successful season under this title was during the 1980-81 season when they lost a two legged final 3-2 on aggregate (0-2, 2-1) to Altrincham. Prior to that Kettering reached the semi-final the previous season losing 3-1 to Northwich Victoria. The Alliance

Premier League Cup gave way to the Bob Lord Trophy for the onset of the 1983-84 season.

ALLIANCE PREMIER LEAGUE SHIELD. Kettering competed against Altrincham during the 1981-82 season, after finishing runners up in the Alliance Premier League and Cup the previous season. The game took place at Moss Lane, with the Robins winning 4-2. Kettering's goals came from Stewart Atkins and Alan Guy.

APPLEBY STEVE. Midfield. Born Boston. Previous clubs. Boston United and Bourne Town. A Peter Morris signing from Bourne Town during the summer of 1991. Steve made one substitute appearance against Braintree in the FA Cup 3rd Qualifying Round, a 3-1 success during the 1991-92 campaign.
Debut (FA Cup) v Braintree (h) 05:09:91
Appearances: 1 League: 0   **Goals:** 0
                  Cups   0+1

ARNOLD IAN. Striker. Born Durham. Previous clubs: Middlesbrough, Carlisle United and Stalybridge Celtic. Originally signed as a trainee by Bruce Rioch when he was Middlesbrough's manager. The enigmatic striker was signed for £10,000 from Carlisle United during the 1994-95 season making quite an impression on the Rockingham Road faithful scoring the club's first hat-trick since Jon Graham's trio in 1991, (against Halifax Town) and fully deserved his England call up and place in the Conference team of 1994-95. 1995-96 was a different story, he never recaptured his form of the previous season and moved for a £15,000 fee to Stalybridge Celtic, (a side he had previously played on loan for before his move to the Poppies) in September 1995, after making just six further appearances for Kettering. Ian represented the England semi-professional side on 2 occasions while at Rockingham Road. Later played for Kidderminster Harriers.
GM Vauxhall Conference, debut v Altrincham (h) 17:12:94
Appearances: 39   League 25+3   **Goals:** 16   League 15
                  Cups   11   Cups   1

ASHBY NICK. Full back. Born Northampton. Nick joined the club during the 1993-94 close season from Aylesbury United. He made 93 appearances for the Poppies scoring one goal from a blistering free kick against Dover Athletic; before linking up with his

4

father (Roger) in a £14,000 move to neighbours Rushden & Diamonds during the summer of 1995. Originally a trainee at Nottingham Forest, he also played for Aylesbury United and Rushden Town. Nick's first season with the club was rewarded with an international call-up to the England semi-professional side and FA XI honours. After Rushden & Diamonds Nick played for Burton Albion.

GM Vauxhall Conference, debut v Halifax Town (a) 21:08:93

Appearances: 95   League 76 **Goals:** 1   League 1
Cups   19

ASHBY ROGER. Full back. Born Northampton. Previous club: Northampton Town. Joined Kettering in 1966 becoming a Poppies legend and record all time appearance holder with 662 outings for the club with a goal scoring tally of 96 (although Roger states he has scored 99). Roger was coming to the end of his Poppies career when the Alliance was formed and made only 37 appearances in the Premier League. One of the best, if not the best right back the club has ever seen. Roger's glory days were in the Southern Premier League. Scored his first Alliance goal in the 2-2 away draw at Wealdstone. He left the Poppies to take over as player/manager of Irthlingborough Diamonds at the end of the 1979-80 season. Later managed Rushden & Diamonds in the GMVC.

Southern League Division One, debut v Stevenage (a) 05:01:67
Alliance Premier League, debut v Stafford Rangers (a) 18:08:79

Appearances: 45   League 37 **Goals:** 6   League 5
Cups   8   Cups   1

ASHDJIAN JOHN. Forward. Born Hackney. Previous clubs: Northampton Town and Scarborough. Signed in November during the 1993-94 season by Graham Carr from Scarborough, where he was the leading goalscorer during season 1991-92. Of his eight Kettering appearances only one was a start, against Welling United in the 2-2 draw at Rockingham Road - he was substituted by Jon Graham who scored, earning the Poppies a point. He was never given a real chance to show the Rockingham Road faithful what he could or could not do. Moved on to Corby Town.

GM Vauxhall Conference, debut v Welling United (a) 04:12:93

Appearances: 8   League 1+5   **Goals:** 0
Cups   0+2

ATKINS STEWART. Striker. Previous clubs: St. Albans City, Chesham, Wycombe Wanderers and Dunstable. Signed by Colin Clarke for the Poppies in December 1980 for £4,000 from Dunstable. Almost a goal every other game, something only Carl Alford in recent times has come near to emulating. Unfortunately this big bustling centre forward left Kettering for Barnet in 1982 for a £4,000 fee.

Alliance Premier League, debut v Barnet (a) 17:12:80

Appearances: 60   League 45   ***Goals:*** 31   League 22
Cups   15   Cups   9

ATTENDANCES. Season 1988-89 saw 70,142 supporters watch the Poppies in the GMVC, FA Cup and Trophy at Rockingham Road giving the club an overall average of 2,697. In contrast to that 19,729 at an average of 939 watched the Poppies in the first season of Vauxhall Conference sponsorship in 1986-87, the lowest margin by some way. The highest attendance for a GMVC match at Rockingham Road is 5,020 v Colchester United in 1990-91. The highest away fixture attendance involving the Poppies, also against Colchester United at Layer Road in 1991-92 saw 6,303 turn out. The lowest Rockingham Road Conference attendance is 532 v Cheltenham Town during the 1985-86 campaign and the lowest away attendance, just 219 at the International Stadium, Gateshead in 1984-85. The highest home cup attendance was created in the FA Cup 1st Round against Northampton Town, (then managed by Graham Carr), a massive 6,100, while the highest attendance involving the Poppies in an away tie was at Charlton Athletic in the 4th Round when 16,001 witnessed the Poppies lose narrowly 2-1 against the First Division side, (before the Premiership had been created). Some of the lowest attendances have been recorded in the various guises of the League Cup. 437 v Boston United in 1986-87, 503 v Farnborough Town in 1996-97, 545 v Runcorn in 1983-84 and 556 v Bangor City in 1982-83. The lowest attendance involving the Poppies was just 119 - away at Stewart & Lloyds in the Northants Senior Cup during the 1995-96 campaign.

B

BANCROFT PAUL. Midfield. Born Derby. Previous clubs: Derby County, Northampton Town, Nuneaton Borough, Burton Albion and Crewe Alexandra. Paul was signed from Conference rivals Kidderminster Harriers by Peter Morris, originally on loan. Affectionately known as 'Banners' while with the club, he certainly was the midfield dynamo Peter Morris had needed, but after injury he was never the same. Paul though, is one of the few players to have scored a hat-trick for the club, two of his three goals coming from penalties against Fisher Athletic. He represented the England semi-professional side while with the Poppies. Rejoined Kidderminster during the 1992-93 season, later played for Shepshed Dynamo in the Dr Marten's Midland Division.

GM Vauxhall Conference, debut v Bath City (a) 18:08:90

Appearances: 106   League 78+6   **Goals:** 15 League 15
Cups   22

BANTON GEOFF. Central defender. Born Ashton-Under-Lyne. Previous clubs: Bolton Wanderers, Plymouth Argyle and Fulham. Joined the Poppies in July 1982. Came off the substitutes bench against Worcester City in October 1982, to score 2 goals in a 4-1 win. During the next two weeks he scored the winners against Altrincham and AP Leamington.

Alliance Premier League, debut v Trowbridge Town (h) 14:08:82

Appearances: 52   League 35+4   **Goals:** 14 League 10
Cups   11+2   Cups   4

BARBER FRED*. Born Ferryhill. Previous clubs: Darlington, Everton, Walsall, Peterborough United, Chester City and Blackpool. Goalkeeper who joined the Poppies on loan from Peterborough United during the 1993-94 campaign. Kept up his wearing of a rubber mask during the warm up before a game. Returned to

Peterborough after a short spell. Later played for Kidderminster Harriers in the Conference.

GM Vauxhall Conference, debut v Bromsgrove Rovers (h) 21:11:92

Appearances: 7   League 5

Cups 2

BARKER DEAN. A defender who joined the club from Sudbury Town during Peter Morris's tenure, making four appearances towards the end of the 1991-92 season. Of his four games the Poppies won two, drew one and lost one. The most emphatic win, a 5-0 thrashing of Altrincham.

GM Vauxhall Conference, debut v Bath City (a) 18:04:92

Appearances: 4   League 4   **Goals:** 0

BARNES BOBBY. Winger. Born Kingston. Previous clubs: West Ham United, Scunthorpe United, Aldershot Town, Swindon Town, AFC Bournemouth, Northampton Town, Peterborough United and Partick Thistle. The experienced winger rejoined the club from Scottish club Partick Thistle joining the Graham Carr contingent of ex-Cobblers who won the 1986 Fourth Division Championship, at the Poppies. Bobby didn't shine at Kettering and was soon on his way, not lasting the 1994-95 season.

GM Vauxhall Conference, debut v Southport (h) 27:08:94

Appearances: 9   League 4+5   **Goals:** 0

Cups 0

BARTLETT PAUL. Winger. A Don Masson signing from Boston United during the 1983-84 close season. Paul scored his only goal for the club on the opening day of the 1983-84 season in the 2-3 defeat by Scarborough at Rockingham Road, becoming the 6th Poppies player to score on his league debut since 1979.

Alliance Premier League, debut v Scarborough (h) 20:08:83

Appearances: 10 League 8   **Goals:** 1   League 1

Cups 2

BASTOCK PAUL. Goalkeeper. Born Redditch. Previous clubs: Cambridge United, Bath City, Coventry City and Fisher Athletic. Paul was originally signed on loan from Cambridge United due to an injury to Kevin Shoemake. He never made the number one jersey his and was in and out of Kettering's team almost duelling with Shoemake on a weekly basis at one stage. He must have known his Poppies career was nearing an end after being dropped by Peter Morris after the 1-4 away defeat at Blackburn Rovers. Finished off the season though as the number one. Later joined Morris at Boston United where he was a firm favourite. "Wiggle it, just a little bit".

GM Vauxhall Conference, debut v Yeovil Town (a) 31:03:90

Appearances: 38   League 29
Cups   9

BEASLEY ANDY*. Goalkeeper. Born Sedgley. Previous clubs: Luton Town, Gillingham, Peterborough United and Scarborough. Andy had two spells at the Poppies both of these on loan from Mansfield Town. His first spell came when Harvey Lim, (also on loan) left the club and Kevin Shoemake was recovering from injury during the 1988-89 season. His second period was only a brief one as a knee injury sustained during the 1992-93 FA Cup 1st Round clash against Gillingham put paid to any further games with the Poppies.

GM Vauxhall Conference, debut v Northwich Victoria (a) 04:03:89

Appearances: 11   League 10
Cups   1

BEAVON DAVID.   Winger. Born Nottingham. Previous clubs: Notts County and Lincoln City. Joined the Poppies pre-season 1983 from Lincoln City. Received his marching orders at Bath City in 1984 for offering strong advice to a linesman, then ordered off the bench and forced to sit in the stand. David scored his only goal for the club in the 3-4 home defeat by Nuneaton Borough in 1984.

Alliance Premier League, debut v Scarborough (h) 20:08:83

Appearances: 45   League 35+1   **Goals:** 1   League 1
Cups   8+1

BEECH GLENN. Midfield. Born Peterborough. Previous clubs: Aston Villa, Stamford, Baker Perkins, Rushden Town and Grantham Town. The diminutive midfielder was signed by Peter Morris for £10,000 - then a club record, from Boston United during the 1988-89 season. Glenn showed rare glimpses of his talent and Morris became discontented with the midfielder. Always seemed to score either for or against us in the Boston United fixture.

Debut (FA Trophy) v Basingstoke (a) 14:01:89
GM Vauxhall Conference, debut v Barnet (a) 21:01:89

Appearances: 51   League 33+10   **Goals:** 4   League 2
Cups   6+2   Cups   2

BENJAMIN IAN. Forward. Born Nottingham. Previous clubs: Sheffield United, West Bromwich Albion, Northampton Town, Peterborough United, Cambridge United, Chester City, Exeter City, Southend United, Luton Town, Brentford and Wigan Athletic. A forward with plenty of league experience. Joined the Poppies just before the transfer deadline during the 1995-96 season. Made quite an impact scoring three goals in his first five appearances, all of them spectacular. Released by Gary Johnson and joined Chelmsford City during the 1996-97 close season, but later that same season he returned to Northamptonshire as Corby Town's player/manager. Made one appearance for the Poppies the following season in the FA Cup as emergency cover during an injury crisis.

GM Vauxhall Conference, debut v Dagenham & Redbridge (a) 06:04:96

Appearances: 9 League 6+3   **Goals:** 3   League 3
Cups   0   Cups   0

BENSTEAD GRAHAM. Goalkeeper. Born Sedgley. Originally Graham had been an apprentice at QPR before going on to play for Norwich City, Colchester United, (on Loan) and Sheffield United before a long spell at Brentford. He joined the Poppies midway through the 1993-94 season and became an instant success going on to make many outstanding performances. Tragedy befell the keeper playing against home town club Woking in the Bob Lord Trophy, where he received a serious knee injury that ruined his season. In fact that was the last time he wore a Kettering Town jersey. Out of contract he left the Poppies later joining neighbours Rushden & Diamonds. Whilst with Kettering he represented the England semi-professional side, and was named in the Vauxhall Conference team of the year for 1993-94. Later played for Kingstonian and briefly Brentford.

GM Vauxhall Conference, debut v Runcorn (h) 25:09:93

Appearances: 65   League 56
Cups   9

BERRY STEVE. Midfield. Born Gosport. Signed during the 1996-97 close season from 1995-96 Vauxhall Conference Champions Stevenage Borough by Gary Johnson. Previous clubs: Portsmouth, Aldershot Town, Sunderland, Newport County, Swindon Town, Northampton Town, SV Damstadt (Germany) and Instant Dicts (Hong Kong). As club captain Steve took over as caretaker manager of the Poppies along with Richard Nugent and

10

Kevin Shoemake after the sacking of Gary Johnson in October 1996. After four games in temporary charge he accepted the vacant player/manager position, becoming the Poppies 22nd post war manager, leading the Poppies to safety and 14th position in the league. But the 1997-98 season started off disastrously, 13 league games without a win, bottom of the Conference, a humiliating defeat in the FA Cup at home to Hinckley United, and just 17 points acquired by December 31st 1997 - relegation seemed certain. But under Berry's leadership the club steered itself away from the dreaded drop into non-league obscurity ending up in 14th place and one point more than the previous season. Kettering fans were shocked in April 1998 to hear of the disharmony, allegedly, between the manager and chairman, with Steve Berry's intentions to leave the club at the end of the season printed in the Evening Telegraph for all to read. A sorry end to Berry's first managerial post, especially after the diabolical start to the season. Rejoined Stevenage Borough after leaving the Poppies.

GM Vauxhall Conference, debut v Macclesfield Town (a) 17:08:96

Appearances: 89 League 68+4   ***Goals:*** 6   League 3
                Cups   16+1   Cups   3
Honours won: Northants Hillier Senior Cup - 1996-97, 1997-98.

MANAGERIAL RECORD
October 1996 - May 1998
(*first 4 matches as caretaker manager)

	P	W	D	L	F	A
League	70	24	18	28	88	98
Cups	17	10	1	6	29	25
TOTAL	***87***	***34***	***19***	***34***	***117***	***123***

BIRCH RAY. Defender. An Alan Buckley signing from the youth team during 1987. Made his Conference debut as a substitute in the 1-2 away defeat at Boston United. Ray made his first start in the 0-3 away defeat by Maidstone United.

GM Vauxhall Conference, debut v Boston United (a) 04:04:87

Appearances: 6   League 4+2   **Goals:** 0

Cups   0

BIRCH TERRY. Centre-back. Previous clubs: Hemel Hempstead and Watford. A stop gap player used during the usual mid-season injury crisis. Signed by Gary Johnson during the 1995-96 season made his debut in the Spalding Challenge Cup.

Debut (League Cup) v Slough Town (h) 13:02:96

Appearances: 2   League 0   **Goals:** 0

Cups   1+1

BLACKWELL KEVIN*. Goalkeeper. Born Luton. Previous clubs: Barton Rovers, Barnet, Boston United, Scarborough and Notts County. A Peter Morris loan signing from Notts County during the 1990-91 season. Made his debut for the Poppies in the first league defeat of the season a 1-5 thrashing by Wycombe Wanderers at Adams Park - a run that had stretched 14 games. After that game Kevin went five consecutive games without conceding a goal, playing his part with Chris Neville during a 9 game unbeaten spell. Blackwell was recalled by Notts County for the Christmas period.

GM Vauxhall Conference, debut v Wycombe Wanderers (a) 03:11:90

Appearances: 29   League 24

Cups   5

BLOODWORTH DARREN. Central defender. Born Market Deeping. Previous club: Bourne Town. Signed by Peter Morris during the 1991-92 close season. Darren never established himself under Morris's leadership. Later played for Kings Lynn and Boston United.

GM Vauxhall Conference, debut v Redbridge Forest (a) 24:08:91

Appearances: 16   League 10+3   **Goals:** 0

Cups   3

BOB LORD TROPHY. The Bob Lord Trophy named after Mr Bob Lord who acted as President of the Football League and was a former Chairman of Burnley Football Club, took over from the

Alliance Premier League Cup, (although the actual cup was the same), for the 1983-84 season and continued until 1985-86 before being succeeded by the GMVCC and Club Call Cup competitions. The following three seasons the BLT returned and during the 1992-93 season was sponsored by Drinkwise. For seasons 1993-94 and 1994-95 it was back to just the BLT before handing over the reins to sponsors Spalding, hence the Spalding Challenge Cup in 1995-96. Under the BLT guise the Poppies reached the final on one occasion, being humbled by Bromsgrove Rovers 10-2 on aggregate in the 1994-95 two legged affair - possibly the worst result in a National Cup Final? (Also see Alliance Premier League Cup).

BOLTON IAN. Central defender. Born Leicester. Previous clubs: Barnet, Notts County, Brentford and Watford. Joined Kettering from Barnet in October 1984. Ian scored his only goal for the club in the 5-0 thrashing of Frickley Athletic, the penultimate home game of the 1984-85 season.

Debut (FA Cup) v Harrow Borough (h) 27:10:84
Gola League, debut v Frickley Athletic (a) 03:11:84
Appearances: 39   League 28 **Goals:** 1   League 1
Cups   11

BOON ROY. Striker. Signed from United Counties League side Stotfold having previously played for Letchworth Garden City. Made two brief appearances against Runcorn and Boston United both at Rockingham Road during the 1989-90 season. Was unfortunate to be in the same squad as Robbie Cooke and Ernie Moss who were at their prime with the Poppies.

GM Vauxhall Conference, debut v Runcorn (h) 26:08:89
Appearances: 2 League 0+2   **Goals:** 0
Cups   0

BOWLING IAN*. Goalkeeper. Born Sheffield. Previous clubs: Frecheville, Stafford Rangers, Gainsborough Trinity and Lincoln City. Signed on loan from Lincoln City during the 1989-90 season. Both of his appearances were away from home. Conceded six goals in his two matches for the Poppies - a defeat and a draw. Later played for Mansfield Town.

GM Vauxhall Conference, debut v Barnet (a) 17:02:90
Appearances: 2   League 2
Cups   0

BOYD WILLIE. Goalkeeper. Born Hamilton. Previous clubs: Hull City, Doncaster Rovers and Grantham. Joined Kettering in October 1984 from Grantham. During the 1984-85 season Willie kept duelling with Nick Goodwin for the keepers jersey.

Gola League, debut v Telford United (h) 03:10:84

Appearances: 33   League 27
                       Cups   6

BRACE MARK. Striker. Brought into Steve Berry's side during the 1997-98 season from local Sunday football.

Debut (League Cup) v Dover Athletic (a) 07:10:97

Appearances: 1   League 0   **Goals:** 0
                     Cup   1

BRADD LES. Forward. Born Buxton, Derbyshire. Previous clubs: Notts County, Stockport County and Wigan Athletic. A Don Masson signing, Les joined Kettering during the 1983-84 close- season from Wigan.   Scored on his league debut in the 2-3 defeat at Rockingham Road by Scarborough, scoring his three goals in his first six games for the club. Beset with injuries throughout his short Poppies career, Bradd's last game for the Poppies was against Weymouth on the last day of 1983. The Poppies drew 1-1 with a goal from Dougie Keast.

Alliance Premier League, debut v Scarborough (h) 20:08:83

Appearances: 17 League 12   **Goals:** 3   League 2
                    Cups   4+1   Cups   1

BROOK GARY*. Forward. A loan signing by Peter Morris he made his only appearance, and that lasted 25 minutes due to damaged knee ligaments, against Stafford Rangers in the 0-0 draw at Marston Road, during the 1990-91 season. Later played for Halifax Town in the GMVC.

GM Vauxhall Conference, debut v Stafford Rangers (a) 30:03:91

Appearances: 1 League 1   **Goals:** 0
                  Cups   0

BROTHERS. The only brothers to play for the Poppies since 1979 are Andy and Mark Harrison. Andy, a winger, played all his games, (23 consecutively), during the 1985-86 season, while goalkeeper Mark played for two campaigns leaving the club during the 1987-88 close season for Stafford Rangers.

BROWN JIM. Goalkeeper. Previous clubs: Chesterfield, Albion Rovers, Sheffield United and Cardiff City. A Jim Conde signing from Cardiff City during the 1982-83 season after an injury to Steve Conroy. An ex-Scottish international who made 10 Alliance Premier League appearances, but failed to keep a clean sheet.

Alliance Premier League, debut v Frickley Athletic (a) 19:03:83

Appearances: 18   League 10

Cups   8

BROWN PHIL. Striker. Born Sheffield. Previous clubs: Chesterfield, Stockport County and Lincoln City. Phil almost became a National Institution during his first spell at the club. He

PHIL BROWN TESTIMONIAL
Rockingham Road, Kettering
Mon 6th May 1996
K.O. 7.30pm

Official Programme £1.20

was signed during the 1990-91 close season by Peter Morris - a very shrewd acquisition. 'Brownie' scored many memorable goals, none more so than the strike at Ewood Park against Blackburn Rovers in the now famous 1-4 defeat in the 3rd Round of the FA Cup. It came as quite a shock to many of the Rockingham Road faithful when he was released at the end of the 1994-95 campaign and later joined Boston United, the team he scored against to ensure our Conference survival during the 1992-93 season, whilst sending the Pilgrims to almost certain relegation at the same time - Boston were in fact relegated that season! He concluded his Poppies career in typical style with a goal in the 4-2 win at Bromsgrove Rovers on the final Saturday of the 1994-95 league season. Phil was granted a Testimonial game at Rockingham Road at the end of the 1995-96 season, a Kettering Town XI v Boston United XI, and playing for both sides the Poppies won 3-2, with Phil scoring both of Boston's goals in the second half, after setting up Kettering's first goal in the first half. Later played for Gainsborough Trinity. After three seasons away from Rockingham

Road, Phil was brought back to the Poppies by Peter Morris in June 1998.

Debut (Maunsell Cup) v Peterborough United (h) 14:08:90
GM Vauxhall Conference, debut v Bath City (a) 18:08:90

Appearances: 244   League 174+17   **Goals:** 68   League 51
            Cups   49+4   Cups   17

BROWN RICHARD. Full back. Born Nottingham. Previous clubs: Derry, Ilkeston Town, Grantham, Boston United, Sheffield Wednesday, Blackburn Rovers, Maidstone United, Stockport County and Blackpool. A Peter Morris signing from Boston United. Known to the fans as 'Bomber'. He made impressive strides that eventually saw a £15,000 move to Blackburn Rovers. Richard played for Rovers against Kettering in Blackburn's 4-1 FA Cup 3rd Round win at Ewood Park. Was brought back to Rockingham Road during the 1995-96 season, by Gary Johnson, but after only one game he suffered an injury outside football that curtailed his comeback. Speedy and influential full-back who could also play in the centre of defence. Later played for Halifax Town and Altrincham.

GM Vauxhall Conference, debut v Maidstone United (a) 12:12:87

Appearances: 89 League 61+2 **Goals:** 2 League 0
Cups 26 Cups 2

BROWN SIMON. Forward. Born Market Harborough. Simon was a product of the youth and reserve sides. He was originally recommended to Kettering after having trials with Leicester City. Joined the club during pre-season 1983 making his only start for the club against Wealdstone in January 1984 - the Poppies lost 2-4.

Debut (FA Trophy) v Dulwich Hamlet (a) 17:12:83
Alliance Premier League, debut v Wealdstone (h) 26:12:83

Appearances: 7 League 1+6 **Goals:** 0
Cups 0+1

BROWNE SHAUN*. Defender. A loan signing from Notts County, made both of his appearances in the BLT semi-final against Sutton United during the 1990-91 season - the Poppies losing 1-4 at Gander Green and the 1-2 defeat by Rushden Town in the Northants Senior Cup semi-final.

Debut (League Cup) v Sutton United (a) 04:04:91

Appearances: 2 League 0 **Goals:** 0
Cups 2

BROWNRIGG ANDREW*. Central defender. Born Sheffield. Signed on loan from Norwich City during the 1995-96 season after a £100,000 transfer from Hereford United. Unfortunately he was injured during his third game at Bath City. Rejoined the club in January 1996, but injury again curtailed his career with the Poppies.

GM Vauxhall Conference, debut v Dover Athletic (a) 02:12:95

Appearances: 4   League 3   *Goals:* 0
                      Cups   1

BRYANT STEVE. A product of the Kettering youth team, Steve was introduced to the first team by Colin Clarke during the 1981-82 season and is one of the very few players to make all his appearances as a substitute - the first against Runcorn at Canal Street, the Linnets winning 3-2.

Alliance Premier League, debut v Runcorn (a) 13:03:82

Appearances: 7   League 0+7   *Goals:* 0
                      Cups   0

BUTTERWORTH GARY*. Midfield. Born Peterborough. Signed on loan from Peterborough United during the 1991-92 season by Peter Morris. Proved to be quite a find, but didn't stay long owing to the interest shown by a number of league clubs, later played for Dagenham & Redbridge. Gary's only goal for the club was scored against Telford United at Bucks Head. Later played in the GMVC for Rushden & Diamonds.

GM Vauxhall Conference, debut v Welling United (a) 11:03:92

Appearances: 8   League 8   *Goals:* 1   League 1
                      Cups   0   Cups   0

BUCKLEY ALAN. Manager. Appointed in November 1986. Alan was the former player/manager of Walsall in 1979, then the youngest player-manager in the Football League. He made Football League appearances for Nottingham Forest, Birmingham City and Walsall. Buckley joined Kettering after being released by Walsall, and so began the re-emergence of Kettering Town Football Club as a force to be reckoned with. Buckley was the last manager to win a major trophy with the Poppies the 1987 GMAC Cup, a 3-1 win over Hendon. Certainly it was a major blow to the club when, during the close season of 1988-89, he moved to Grimsby Town, taking Arthur

Mann, Paul Reece and Andy Tillson to Blundell Park. Under Buckley the club finished the 1987-88 season in third place, the highest position since the runners-up position in 1980-81.

Honours won: GMAC Cup, 1986-87.
Northants Senior Cup, 1986-87.
Maunsell Cup, 1987-88.

MANAGERIAL RECORD
November 1986 to June 1988

	P	W	D	L	F	A
League	67	30	17	20	101	81
Cups	24	13	4	7	41	28
TOTAL	*91*	*43*	*21*	*27*	*142*	*109*

C

CARTER RECKEY. Striker. Previous clubs: Bromsgrove Rovers, Solihull Borough, Malvern Town, Worcester City, Kidderminster Harriers, Fairfield and Northfield Town. Signed for the Poppies during the 1996-97 close season for £20,000 from Bromsgrove Rovers where he scored 78 goals in 128 appearances. Unfortunately Reckey never lived up to his reputation, scoring just 2 goals, (against Atherstone United in the FA Cup), in 11 appearances before a strange move in October 1996 to a former club Solihull Borough - two divisions lower, for £17,500.

GM Vauxhall Conference, debut v Macclesfield Town (a) 17:08:96

Appearances: 11　　League 8　**Goals:** 2　League 0
Cups　2+1　　　　　　　　Cups　2

CARR GRAHAM. Former manager of Weymouth, Dartford, Nuneaton Borough, Northampton Town, Maidstone United and Blackpool. Graham took over as manager of Kettering Town during the 1992-93 season, when the club was in extreme difficulty, not only on the pitch but off it. With the threat of a winding up order hanging over the club virtually everyday and with little money to spend to assemble a team to keep the club in the GMVC, Carr worked wonders that season along with assistant Clive Walker after Dave Cusack's eight game (Mark English) tenure. The Poppies, second from bottom and likely favourites for the drop, recovered to a respectable 13th position by the end of the season. When chairman Peter Mallinger stepped in the following season, Carr's new team ran out just three points short of promotion to the Football League. A 6th position was recorded the following season in the league and a Bob Lord Trophy final defeat at the hands of Bromsgrove Rovers, surprisingly saw much unrest at the club. Carr left at the end of the 1994-95 season and took over the managers chair - briefly, four days later at Weymouth. For a season and a half Graham Carr was a cult hero with the Poppies fans, but as results, gates, and patience wore thin, the writing was on the wall. Later he became the manager of Dagenham & Redbridge.

Honours won: Northants Senior Cup, 1992-93.
Maunsell Cup, 1993-94.

MANAGERIAL RECORD
September 1992 to May 1995

	P	W	D	L	F	A
League	120	50	37	33	179	136
Cups	29	12	5	12	48	52
TOTAL	**149**	**62**	**42**	**45**	**227**	**188**

Graham Carr worked miracles during the 1992-93 season.

CAVENER PHIL. Midfield. Born North Shields. Previous clubs: Burnley, Bradford City, Gillingham, Northampton Town and Peterborough United. He signed for Southend United during the summer of 1986 but later decided to go part-time with the Poppies. Phil's Poppies career was cut short during the final week of the 1986-87 season when he was seriously injured in a car crash, he was never to play for Kettering again. Scored his first goals, a brace, against Welling United in the Poppies 5-1 home win, still the club's best result against the Kent club. The club played a Benefit match for Phil against West Bromwich Albion during April 1988.

GM Vauxhall Conference, debut v Frickley Athletic (a) 09:09.86

Appearances: 38   League 25+1   **Goals:** 5   League 4
Cups 12   Cups 1

CHAIRMEN. Since 1979 the following have all been chairman of Kettering Town Football Club. Tom Bradley, John Murphy, Nev Tingle, Cyril Gingell, Merv Baxter, Jim Lynch (twice), Brian Talbot, Mark English, Peter Mallinger.

Current chairman Peter Mallinger bought Kettering Town Football Club after much negotiation from administrators, Panel, Kerr & Foster after the 1992-93 season, just in time as it turned out for the following 1993-94 campaign. Effectively he ensured the future of the Poppies after the previous back room set up almost put the club out of business. A vast injection of capital, hard work and dedication by the ex-Newcastle United vice-chairman put the Poppies back on a sound footing.

CHAMBERLAIN GLYN. Central defender. Born Chesterfield. Previous clubs: Burnley, Chesterfield and Halifax Town. Joined the Poppies from the Shaymen (Halifax Town) during the summer of 1982. Scored his only league goal against Dagenham in the Poppies 3-2 win at Victoria Road in September 1982.

Alliance Premier League, debut v Trowbridge Town (h) 14:08:82

Appearances: 86 League 65+4   **Goals:** 2   League 1
Cups 16+1   Cups 1

CHAPMAN CAMPBELL. Made just two Vauxhall Conference appearances during the 1986-87 season. Left the Poppies for Altrincham during Alan Buckley's tenure.

GM Vauxhall Conference, debut v Dagenham (a)14:03:87

Appearances: 2   League 1+1   **Goals:** 0
Cups 0

CHARD PHIL. Midfield. Born Corby. Previous clubs: Northampton Town, Peterborough United and Wolverhampton Wanderers. Joined the Poppies originally at the start of the 1994-95 pre-season, but was injured in a friendly before the season got underway. Rejoined the club in December making his debut against

Woking in the BLT quarter final replacing Anton Thomas. Constant injury niggles forced the ex-Northampton Town player/manager to play little part in Graham Carr's plans.

Debut (League Cup) v Woking (h) 20:12:94
GM Vauxhall Conference, debut v Dagenham & Redbridge (a) 31:12:94
Appearances: 10   League 6   **Goals:** 0
Cups   2+2

CHERRY STEVE. Goalkeeper. Born Nottingham. Previous clubs: Derby County, Port Vale, Walsall, Plymouth Argyle (twice), Chesterfield, Notts County, Watford and Rotherham United. Experienced football league goalkeeper who made the majority of his appearances for Notts County. Signed by Steve Berry on a non-contract basis during the 1996-97 season during another goalkeeping crisis, making three appearances, including a super display against Rushden & Diamonds that prompted the Nene Park club to make him an offer 48 hours later that, allegedly, he could not refuse. Later played for Stalybridge Celtic.

GM Vauxhall Conference, debut v Altrincham (h) 11:03:97
Appearances: 3   League 3
Cups   0

CHESHIRE BLAIR. Forward. Made his four appearances during the 1981-82 campaign, the first game at Runcorn's Canal Street. Blair was not on a winning side for the Poppies. The 1-1 draw at Stafford Rangers was the teams best result during his short stint in the team.

Alliance Premier League, debut v Runcorn (a) 13:03:82
Appearances: 5 League 3+1   **Goals:** 0
Cups   1

CHILDS GARY. Gary's only appearance came as a substitute for David Hofbauer during the 1983-84 match against Yeovil Town at the Huish. The Glovers won 2-0.

Alliance Premier League, debut v Yeovil Town (a) 02:08:84
Appearances: 1   League 0+1   **Goals:** 0
Cups   0

CHRISTIE TREVOR. Striker. Born Newcastle. Previous clubs: Mansfield Town, Walsall, Manchester City, Derby County, Nottingham Forest, Notts County and Leicester City. The experienced traveller, joined the Poppies from Mansfield Town during the summer of 1991, scoring on his debut for the club in the 1-1 draw at Altrincham on the opening day of the 1991-92 season, the fifth Kettering player to do since Billy Jeffrey in season 1984-85. Chipped in with the odd goal now and again - two during the infamous 1991-92 FA Cup run, against Stafford Rangers and Wycombe Wanderers. After leaving the Poppies Trevor joined VS Rugby.

GM Vauxhall Conference, debut v Altrincham (a) 17:08:91

Appearances: 34 League 19+2   **Goals:** 8   League 5
Cups   11+2   Cups   3

CLARKE   COLIN.

Player/Manager.

Previous club: Oxford United - where he made over 500 appearances Also played for Arsenal, Los Angeles Aztex and Plymouth Argyle. Colin joined Kettering for the start of the 1979-80 season after the departure of Mick Jones to Mansfield Town. Clarke was left with a depleted squad due to injury and suspension plus, he had to follow in the only manager footsteps that had taken the Club to a Wembley Final. Colin's first game in charge ironically was against Stafford Rangers in the newly formed Alliance Premier League, just a few weeks after the Poppies FA Trophy defeat. This time though, the result was a 0-0 draw at Marston Road. Clarke's best season in charge was the 1980-81 campaign when the Poppies finished three points behind Altrincham to end in the runners-up postion. This would not be achieved again until eight seasons later. Clarke became the first Kettering manager to win two Manager of the Month awards. Neither of his Alliance Premier League goals were scored at Rockingham Road, the first in a 2-1 away win at Worcester City and the second in the 5-1 demolition of Nuneaton Borough. Colin later managed Stafford Rangers in the Alliance Premier League.

Alliance Premier League, debut v Stafford Rangers (a) 18:09:79
Appearances: 97 League 75   **Goals:** 3   League 2
               Cups   21+1   Cups   1
Honours won: Northants Senior Cup. 1979-80.

MANAGERIAL RECORD
August 1979 to February 1982

	P	W	D	L	F	A
League	101	41	31	29	158	129
Cups	29	13	6	10	45	38
TOTAL	**130**	**54**	**37**	**39**	**203**	**167**

CLARKE PETER. Defender. Made his Poppies league debut in the 2-3 defeat at Canal Street, Runcorn during the 1981-82 season. Played three straight games, without being on the winning side, then that was his lot.

Alliance Premier League, debut v Runcorn (a) 13:03:82
Appearances: 3   League 3   **Goals:** 0
             Cups   0

CLARKE SIMON. Centre-back. Born Chelmsford. Originally signed on loan from West Ham United during the 1992-93 season by Graham Carr. Simon never realised the potential he showed in his early games with the club and, although he chipped in with the odd goal now and again, he never was the force he could have been. Once took over in goal for Graham Benstead after he had been sent off against Welling United in 1993-94. Simon's first action was to face a penalty - he made a valiant effort - the ball was adjudged to have crossed the line after his brave attempt at keeping it out. Welling won controversially 2-0.

GM Vauxhall Conference, debut v Welling United (h) 05:12:92
Appearances: 74   League 47+12   **Goals:** 5   League 4
             Cups   12+3   Cups   1

CLAYTON ROY. Striker. Born Dudley (West Midlands). Probably the best goalscorer the club has ever seen. Roy was signed by Ron Atkinson from Oxford United in a £10,000 deal during 1972. The clubs all time record goal scorer with 171 (1972-1981). He only made 33 Alliance Premier League appearances, scoring 12 goals. Like Roger Ashby, Roy's glory days with the Poppies were in the Southern Premier League. He did score the club's first ever goal in the Alliance Premier, in-fact a brace against

Wealdstone in the Poppies 2-0 home win. Roy was member of the England non-league 1979-80 squads that faced Scotland and Holland. He left Kettering in August 1980 for Barnet but was soon back in the county with Corby Town.

Southern Premier League, debut v Nuneaton Borough (h) 06:11:72
Alliance Premier League, debut v Stafford Rangers (a) 18:08:79

Appearances: 40   League 33 **Goals:** 15 League 12
                       Cups 7   Cups   3

CLUB CALL CUP. A one season sponsorship of the League Cup (and new title) in 1988-89. The Poppies lost in the 2nd Round 0-3 to Leytonstone-Ilford at Green Pond Road in front of the lowest away gate involving Kettering, in a major competition. Just 206 turned out. The previous round at Worksop had attracted just 356.

CLUB SPONSORS. In the past the club's main sponsor's have been, T & K Home Improvements, Britannia Glass, MILAS, PHS (medical services), Healthcrafts, RCI, Fenner Power Transmission and Polar Trucks.

COLLIER GRAHAM. Signed from Boston United during August 1982. Graham scored a superb goal in his last game for the club against Bath City in September 1982, a day after he was told he was not wanted by Kettering.

Alliance Premier League, debut v Trowbridge Town (h) 14:08:82

Appearances: 9   League 3+4 **Goals:** 2   League 2
                      Cups   1+1

COLLINS STEVE. Full back. Born Stamford. Previous clubs: Peterborough United (twice), Southend United and Lincoln City. Steve was a Peter Morris signing during the 1989-90 close season from Peterborough United. A gritty performer, Steve was a popular player during his time with the club winning both the Player and the Player's Player of the Year for 1989-90. After leaving Kettering in 1991 he joined Boston United.

GM Vauxhall Conference, debut v Runcorn (h) 26:08:89

Appearances: 70   League 56+1 **Goals:** 3 League 3
                       Cups   12+1

CONROY STEVE*. Goalkeeper. Previous clubs: Leeds United and Rotherham United. A Jim Conde signing on loan from Rotherham United during February 1983. Made his league debut against Stafford Rangers at Marston Road in the Poppies 1-1 draw. Steve was injured playing for Rotherham reserves just before the Poppies fixture at West Field Lane, Frickley. He conceded 4 goals in his three matches with the Poppies. Two draws and one defeat.

Alliance Premier League, debut v Stafford Rangers (a) 26:02:83

Appearances: 3 League 3
         Cups 0

Jim Conde

CONDE JIM. Took over as manager in the wake of Colin Clarke's shock decision to take over as the new Corby Town manager in February 1982. Prior to his new post Conde was Clarke's assistant and a former striker for the club during the Southern Premier days. He led the club through one of its most traumatic periods not only on the pitch but off it - almost as dire as the 1992-93 season. In the end Chairman John Murphy decided to sack Conde after a series of poor results during March 1983, bringing in former Scottish International midfielder Don Masson as his replacement.

MANAGERIAL RECORD
February 1982 to March 1983

	P	W	D	L	F	A
League	51	12	11	28	81	113
Cups	11	4	3	4	17	23
TOTAL	**62**	**16**	**14**	**32**	**105**	**136**

COOKE ROBBIE. Striker. Born Rotherham. Previous clubs: Mansfield Town, Grantham Peterborough United, Cambridge United, Brentford and Millwall. Another superb finisher. A gem of a signing from Millwall by Peter Morris in 1988. Cooke was inspirational during his first season with a brilliant array of goals in the league, he also went on to score 11 goals during the 1988-89 FA Cup run, the country's leading cup scorer. Cooke's efforts in 1989-90 were rewarded with 28 league goals and the Mail On Sunday prestigious title of 'Goalscorer of the Year'. Robbie formed a great partnership with the experienced Ernie Moss, to date there hasn't been a pair like them. Robbie, was typical of Alan Clarke's nickname 'Sniffer'. I always felt we had a chance if we were down and Cooke was playing, like Frankie Murphy he could conjure up a goal out of nothing with ease. Robbie's last game for the club was as a substitute on the final day of the 1990-91 season during the 1-1 draw at Rockingham Road against Yeovil Town. After leaving Kettering he rejoined former club Grantham Town. Later managed Warboys Town, before returning to Kettering as Peter Morris' assistant in May 1998.

GM Vauxhall Conference, debut v Wycombe Wanderers (h) 10:09:88
Appearances: *120* League 93+2   **Goals:** 60 League 49
Cups   24+1   Cups   11

COSTELLO PETER*. Striker. Born Halifax. Previous clubs: Bradford City, Rochdale, Peterborough United, Lincoln City, Telford United and Dover Athletic. Originally signed on loan from Lincoln City during the 1993-94 season by Graham Carr. Made an immediate impact by scoring the equaliser against Kidderminster Harriers in the 1-1 draw at Rockingham Road. In his six league games he scored in three of the first four. If Peter had been signed earlier in the season the Poppies would have probably won the league. A disappointing end came when playing against Rushden & Diamonds in the Northamptonshire Senior Cup semi-final, he was blatantly fouled, dislocating his shoulder and other than a brief pre-season run about in 1995-96, was never seen in Kettering's colours again until Steve Berry's tenure as manager when he brought the striker back on a non-contract basis in August 1997. Peter repaid his boss' faith by scoring on his second home debut in the 3-3 draw against Slough Town at Rockingham Road. Went on to score 6 more important goals during the difficult 1997-98 campaign.

GM Vauxhall Conference, debut v Kidderminster Harriers (h) 05:03:94

Appearances: 50   League 37+3   **Goals:** 10 League 9
                     Cups   9+1   Cups   1

COTTON PERRY. Striker. Born Chislehurst. Previous clubs: Scunthorpe United, Matlock Town, Goole Town and Nelson United (NZ). A New Zealand International who was signed by Peter Morris from Scunthorpe United during the 1991-92 close season. Made his debut on the opening day of the season at Altrincham (1-1), playing the first four games of the season in which the Poppies won none. His final appearance in a Kettering shirt came as a substitute, the Poppies going down 2-3 to Slough Town, the 'Rebels' only success to date at Rockingham Road.

GM Vauxhall Conference, debut v Altrincham (a) 17:08:91

Appearances: 9   League 4+2   **Goals:** 0
                    Cups   1+2

COX PAUL*. Defender. Born Nottingham. Signed on loan originally by Peter Morris from Notts County. He made just one appearance for the Poppies before returning to County. Rejoined Kettering twice during the 1995-96 season from Notts County and Burnley after spending a loan period with Hull City, whilst on Notts' books. Later played for Halifax Town in the GMVC before returning again to the Poppies for a fourth time in 1997-98 under Steve Berry's management.

GM Vauxhall Conference, debut v Northwich Victoria (h) 17:03:91

Appearances: 37   League 25+3   **Goals:** 0
                     Cups   8+1

CRABB NEIL. Full back. Born Kettering. Neil was a product of the Kettering Town youth setup making his debut at Rockingham Road against Kidderminster Harriers (4-2) during the 1983-84 season. A knee injury forced him out of the Poppies side after just a few appearances.

Alliance Premier League, debut v Kidderminster Harriers (h) 24:03:84

Appearances: 5   League 4   **Goals:** 0

Cups   1

CRAWLEY IAN. Striker. Born Coventry. Affectionately known and remembered by the Poppies faithful as 'Creepy'. Previous clubs, Nuneaton Borough, Bedworth and VS Rugby. Joined the Poppies for £2,000 from VS Rugby during the 1985-86 pre-season, quite a fee when you consider the club was over £100,000 in debt at the time. Scored in his third game for the Poppies in the 3-0 away win at Nuneaton Borough. Also scored in both games against Boston United, accumulating with a hat-trick on the 1st day of 1986 as the Poppies avenged their 1-4 Boxing day defeat, with a 3-1 win at Rockingham Road. Crawley also went on to score five goals in three matches during April before a 15 match run without a goal. Ian was sold for £6,000 to Telford United, after scoring a goal in the 3-0 Maunsell Cup victory over Peterborough during August 1988.

Gola League, debut v Altrincham (a) 24:08:85

Appearances: 100   League 56+22   **Goals:** 30   League 24

Cups   17+ 5   Cups   6

CREANE GED. Central defender. Born Lincoln. Previous clubs: Lincoln City, Tsun Wan (Hong Kong) and Boston United. A Peter Morris signing during the 1988-89 season from Boston United. After barely a season and, due to work commitments, left during the 1989-90 close season. His only goal for the club came in the 2-0 win against Cheltenham Town at Rockingham Road.

GM Vauxhall Conference, debut v Macclesfield Town (a) 12:11:88

Appearances: 26   League 24   **Goals:** 1   League 1

Cups   2

CREASER GLYN. Central defender. Born London. Previous clubs: Wolverton, Northampton Town and Barnet. Signed by Don Masson from Wolverton during the 1983-1984 season. After a club suspension he was to play just two more games for the Poppies. Later played for the Wycombe Wanderers side that won the GMVC.

Even later had a brief spell at neighbours Rushden & Diamonds and Dagenham & Redbridge.

Alliance Premier League, debut v Altrincham (h) 31:03:84

Appearances: 9   League 8   **Goals:** 0
Cups   1

CULLIP DANNY*. Centre-back. Signed on loan during the 1995-96 season, but was recalled by Oxford United after only a few games. In only his second game (Morecambe), he received a head injury that needed a number of stitches - that led to Craig Norman making his debut after only 24 minutes of the game. Later played for Fulham in the Nationwide League.

GM Vauxhall Conference, debut v Slough Town (h) 07:10:95

Appearances: 3   League 3   **Goals:** 0
Cups   0

CULPIN PAUL*. Striker. Born Kirby Muxloe. Previous clubs: Nuneaton Borough, Coventry City, Northampton Town (twice) and Peterborough United. Also played five times for the England semi-professional side. The goal scoring legend from Nuneaton's past only found the net once during his short spell with the Poppies and that was against Bashley in the fog bound FA Trophy 2nd Round 3-2 success in 1992.

GM Vauxhall Conference, debut v Colchester United (h) 24:01:92

Appearances: 7   League 4   **Goals:** 1   League 0
Cups   3   Cups   1

CUNNINGHAM JAMIE. Forward. A prolific goalscorer with United Counties side Cogenhoe United but was given little opportunity making just one substitute appearance during the 1992-93 season against Welling United, the Poppies going down 2-4 at Rockingham Road. The only Poppies player to sport a pony tail! On leaving the Poppies he joined Bugbrooke before a spell at Desborough Town.

GM Vauxhall Conference, debut v Welling United (h) 05:12:92

Appearances: 1   League 0+1   **Goals:** 0
Cups   0

CURTIS ANDY. Winger. Born Doncaster. A Dave Cusack signing from York City during the 1992-93 close season, where he returned after a short spell at Rockingham Road.

GM Vauxhall Conference, debut v Slough Town (a) 22:08:92

Appearances: 6   League 3+3   ***Goals:*** 0
Cups   0

CURTIS BOB. Full back. Previous clubs: Charlton Athletic, Bedford Town, Corby Town and Mansfield Town. Joined the Poppies in the summer of 1980 from Mansfield. Scored on his Alliance debut against Worcester City adding three more goals in the next three games. His final league game for the Poppies was the 1-3 away defeat at Stafford Rangers on the final Saturday of the season. He retired from the game in the close season.

Alliance Premier League, debut v Worcester City (a) 16:08:80
Appearances: 33   League 25   ***Goals:*** 4 League 4
Cups   8

CURTIS HAMISH*. Midfield. Signed by Peter Morris on loan from Peterborough United during the 1991-92 season. Made impressive strides while under Morris but went back to Peterborough to try to reclaim a regular place in the Posh's first team after a run in the Conference. Later played under Morris at Boston United.

GM Vauxhall Conference, debut v Runcorn (h) 15:02:92
Appearances: 19   League 17   ***Goals:*** 0
Cups 2

CURTIS PAUL. Defender. Born London. Previous clubs: Charlton Athletic, Northampton Town and Corby Town. Retired from the game due to increasing work commitments. Paul's only league goal came against Maidstone United in the Poppies 3-2 away win during the 1987-88 campaign.

Debut (Maunsell Cup) v Northampton Town (h) 08:08:87
GM Vauxhall Conference, debut v Enfield (h) 22:08:8 7
Appearances: 21   League 14+1   ***Goals:*** 1 League 1
Cups   5+1

CUSACK DAVID. Born Rotherham. He played for Sheffield Wednesday, Southend United and Millwall, while at Rotherham United and Doncaster Rovers as player/manager. Dave joined Boston United originally as a player, taking over the Pilgrims hot seat after the departure of George Kerr, ironically after our 5-0 thrashing of our Lincolnshire rivals. He joined the Poppies during the 1992-93 close season having left Boston United to replace Peter Morris who had resigned as Poppies manager in the summer.

Morris took over at Cusack's former club Boston, to complete the circle. Cusack took a lot of the flak for Chairman, Mark English who, in the end left the club. We shall never know if Cusack could have done a decent job for the club as he was relieved of his duties by the Administrators Panel, Kerr & Foster after only seven games in charge. Changed the Poppies strip to that of the 1970's era of Red & Black stripes, Black Shorts. Won the Maunsell Cup beating Peterborough United 1-0, with a goal from Dave Riley.

Honours won: Maunsell Cup, 1992-93.

MANAGERIAL RECORD
June to September 1992

	P	W	D	L	F	A
League	6	2	1	3	5	7
Cups	1	1	0	0	1	0
TOTAL	7	3	1	3	6	7

Dave Cusack

D

DALEY STEVE. Previous clubs: Rhyl, Wolverhampton Wanderers, Manchester City and Walsall. Joined the Poppies from Rhyl, where he was the player manager, in January 1987. Manager Alan Buckley was instrumental in bringing the former "£1 million pound man" to Rockingham Road. It was a short stay, as Daley retired from the game during the 1987-88 close season but was then persuaded out of retirement by Buckley during February 1988.

Having scored in the GMAC semi-final against Aylesbury United during his first season with the club, Steve added two Conference goals against Telford United and Wealdstone in consecutive games in March, the Poppies winning both games 3-2. He finally left the Poppies during the 1988-89 close season during the Alan Buckley departure and Peter Morris take over. Later managed Telford United in the Conference.

GM Vauxhall Conference, debut v Northwich Victoria (h) 24:01:87
Appearances: 36 League 27+4   **Goals:** 3 League 2
Cups   5   Cups   1

DAWSON DICK. Striker. Born Chesterfield. Previous clubs: Rotherham United, Doncaster Rovers, Chesterfield, Scarborough and Gainsborough Trinity. Joined the Poppies in March 1984. Never a consistent goalscorer he opened his account with three goals in a four game spell during April 1984, the first against Bath

City in the 1-1 draw. He was released by Alan Buckley during the 1986-87 season and joined Matlock Town.

Alliance Premier League, debut v Altrincham (h) 31:03:84

Appearances: 106   League 69+11   **Goals:** 8   League 5
                       Cups   23+3   Cups   3

DEBUTS. Every new season the opening day game could produce a number of debutee's, depending on who has joined the club during the close season. The record number to make their debuts on the opening day, so far is 10, on August 22nd 1992. They are; Shane Reddish, Irvin Gernon, Christopher Swailes, Ian Docker, David Tomlinson, Steve Adams, David Riley, Shaun Sowden, *Andy Curtis and *Glen Russell, (*both coming on as substitutes) - the Poppies lost 0-3 at Slough Town. Only Paul Nicol and Phil Brown remained from the 1991-92 side, the goalkeeper that day was the returning, Paul Reece, who last played for the Poppies during the 1987-88 season. In contrast to all that activity, during the inaugural season 1979-80, Colin Clarke was the only player to make his debut, (as a substitute), on the opening day.

The most number of players to make their debuts for the Poppies during a season is 40, under the Dave Cusack, Graham Carr 1992-93 season, just 10 more than Gary Johnson's 1995-96 campaign These statistics do not include the Northants Senior Cup or Maunsell Cup.

Altrincham are the most popular side for Poppies players making their debuts against, with 39 taking their first tentative steps against the Robins. Next in line are Cheshire rivals Runcorn, with 18 Poppies making their debuts.

Technically Kevin Shoemake has made three debuts for Kettering, making his first and the one that counts against Northwich Victoria in 1988-89. After leaving the club his second debut was against Altrincham at Moss Lane on the opening day of the 1991-92 season - he ended the season playing against the Poppies for Redbridge Forest at Rockingham Road (the Poppies won 3-2). During the 1992-93 close season he returned to the fold and played in the pre-season friendlies but opted for Rushden & Diamonds as he wasn't offered a contract with the Poppies. Finally he made his third comeback debut as a substitute for the injured Alan Judge again against Altrincham at Moss Lane in 1995-96.

DEBUT GOALS. Since the formation of the Alliance Premier League, 30 players have scored on their first class Kettering Town debuts, the first being Doug Hickton, whose goal was enough to beat Barnet 1-0 during season 1979-80. Mark Smith and Marc North scored twice on their debuts, while North, also with David Hodges and Mick Vinter, did so as a substitute. The full list of players in order are; Doug Hickton, Bob Curtis, Stewart Atkins (APLC), Terry Goode, Les Bradd, Paul Bartlett, Doug Keast, Billy Jeffrey, Maurice Muir, Mark Smith, Mick Vinter, Cohen Griffith, Les Lawrence, David Ritchie, Paul Emson (BLT), Trevor Christie, Richard Walker, Pat Gavin, Marc North, Micky Nuttell, David Riley (MCF), Tony Loughlan (MCF), Chris Hope, David Hodges, Adrian Thorpe, Peter Costello, Johnny Magee (BLT), Jamie Woodsford, Chris Pearson, Sven Sinden (NSC).

DEFEATS. The first defeat in the Alliance Premier came after an eight game unbeaten spell. Bath City inflicted a 2-1 home defeat on Saturday 22nd September 1979. The Poppies went almost four months before the first away defeat, at the hands of Scarborough. The Yorkshire side winning 2-0 on Saturday 3rd November 1979. The heaviest defeat since 1979 was recorded at Gander Lane, in a GMVC match against Sutton United - the Poppies going down 0-8. The heaviest home defeat came in the FA Cup 1st Round in 1983-84 when Swindon Town inflicted a 0-7 thrashing. The worst home defeat in the league was the final home game of the 1995-96 season when Stalybridge Celtic inflicted a 1-6 thrashing. The Poppies ended the 1995-96 season with eight consecutive defeats the worst sequence in the clubs history - which overlapped to the 1996-97 season with a further two more defeats, ten in total. The most league defeats during a season was 24 in 1982-83, the most home league defeats, 9 in 1983-84 and the most away defeats, 17 in 1982-83.

DEMPSEY MARK*. Winger. Born Dublin. Irish winger who came on loan from Gillingham towards the end of the 1993-94 season. Struck up a good understanding with another loanee Peter Costello, but injury to both of them at a vital stage during the final weeks of the season - Mark with a neck injury ended the Poppies hopes. Scored one of his goals with a blistering 30 yard free kick against Bromsgrove Rovers in the Poppies 4-0 away win. Rejoined Gillingham at the end of his loan period, later played for Leyton Orient and Shrewsbury Town.

36

GM Vauxhall Conference, debut v Kidderminster Harriers (h) 05:03:94
Appearances: 14   League 12   ***Goals:*** 5   League 3
                   Cups   1   Cups   2

DENYER PETER. Midfield. Born Chiddingford, Surrey. Previous clubs: Portsmouth and Northampton Town. Peter joined Kettering in pre-season 1983 working his way up the ladder from playing to coaching the youth set up and in October 1983 he became the assistant manager to Dave Needham. Scored his first Alliance goal in the 1-3 away defeat against Boston United, following that two days later in the 1-1 away draw at Altrincham. Peter's third and final Alliance goal was scored on the 2nd day of 1984 again away from home this time in the 2-4 defeat by Wealdstone. Peter was released during the 1985-86 close season.

Alliance Premier League, debut v Scarborough (h) 20:08:83
Appearances: 94   League 70+4   ***Goals:*** 4   League 3
                   Cups   18+2   Cups   1

DE VITO (GEORGIO) CLAUDIO. Forward. A teenage striker signed by Steve Berry from Northampton Town during the latter stages of the 1996-97 season. Rejoined Kettering's troubled side the following season as a full back. Joined Barnet on transfer deadline day.

GM Vauxhall Conference, debut v Hednesford Town (a) 22:03:97
Appearances: 35   League 19+3   ***Goals:*** 0
                   Cups   12+1

DISCIPLINE. Season 1995-96 saw the club's worst disciplinary record, with 15 players sent off in first class action and the worst number of penalty points and bookings in British senior football. The club was fined £7,000, of which £5,000 was suspended until the end of 1996-97.

DIVER SHAUN. Striker. A product of the Poppies youth system and introduced into the first team by Jim Conde making his Alliance debut in the 0-6 away thrashing by Runcorn, during the 1982-83 season - the Poppies second worst league result since 1979. Shaun scored both of his goals in the Northants Senior Cup semi-final against Corby Town, (a team he would later play for), the Poppies won 4-1. Left the Poppies for Desborough Town, Rothwell Town and later Corby Town.

Alliance Premier League, debut v Runcorn (a) 05:10:82

Appearances: 7   League 2+3   **Goals:** 2   League 0
                      Cups   2   Cups   2

DIXEY RICHARD. Centre-back. 'Dixey' is another one of the Poppies who played 99% of his career in the Southern Premier League. He only featured in three Alliance games for Kettering, as a substitute against Altrincham and two starts against Stafford Rangers and Yeovil Town, during the inaugural season. Transferred to Scarborough in 1979.

Southern Premier League, debut v Maidstone United (a) 28:08:76
Alliance Premier League, debut v Altrincham (h) 06:10:79

Appearances: 3   League 2+1   **Goals:** 0
                      Cups   0

DOCKER IAN. Midfield. Born Gravesend. Previous clubs: Gillingham and Redbridge Forest. Joined the Poppies during the 1992-93 season having played for Redbridge Forest previously. Deputised in goal during the 2-3 FA Cup 1st Round defeat against former club Gillingham at the Priestville Stadium, in place of the injured Andy Beasley. Scored his only goal for the Poppies in the spirited 2-2 draw at Northwich Victoria, - Graham Carr's first game in charge of the club.

Debut (Maunsell Cup) v Peterborough United (h) 08:08:92
GM Vauxhall Conference, debut v Slough Town (a) 22:08:92

Appearances: 18   League 14   **Goals:** 1   League 1
                       Cups   3+1

DONALD WARREN. Midfield. Born Uxbridge. This diminutive midfielder joined the Poppies from Colchester United during the 1992-93 season. His career began at West Ham United where he made a couple of first team appearances. He rejoined manager Graham Carr at Kettering having played under him in Northampton Town's Division 4 Championship winning side of 1986. While at Colchester he won the GMVC and FA Trophy. Warren was appointed Club Captain for the season, finishing runners-up to Kidderminster Harriers. He was plagued with injuries at the onset to the 1994-95 season and sustained a broken foot against Macclesfield Town within the first five minutes of his comeback. On leaving the Poppies Warren joined Nuneaton Borough.

GM Vauxhall Conference, debut v Merthyr Tydfil (h) 17:10:92

Appearances: 107   League 80+2   **Goals:** 4   League 3
                        Cups   23+2   Cups   1

38

DONN NIGEL*. Signed on loan from Gillingham during the 1981-82 season by manager Colin Clarke. Later played against the Poppies in the GMVC for Dover Athletic.

Alliance Premier League, debut v Gravesend & Northfleet (h) 10:10:81

Appearances: 4   League 4   **Goals:** 0
Cups   0

DONOVAN NEIL. Signed by Graham Carr from Daventry Town towards the end of the 1992-93 season, scoring his only two goals for the club on the final Saturday of the season in the 2-1 win at Dagenham & Redbridge - denying the Essex club of the runners-up position. He was released the following season and spent a period at Worcester City.

GM Vauxhall Conference, debut v Stalybridge Celtic (a) 17:04:93

Appearances: 10   League 1+6   **Goals:** 2   League 2
Cups   2+1

DOWLING LUKE. Forward. Born Kettering. Signed as an apprentice from the youth team during the 1995-96 season. Went on to make several appearances in his first season and scored his opening goal in the Conference during the 2-3 defeat at Bromsgrove Rovers. Played for Rothwell Corinthians and Corby Town during the 1996-97 season, before making just one substitute appearance for the Poppies. Left the Poppies at the end of the season.

GM Vauxhall Conference, debut v Dover Athletic (a) 02:12:95

Appearances: 7   League 1+5   **Goals:** 2   League 2
Cups   1

DOWNS GREG*. Central defender. Born Charlton. Previous clubs: Norwich City, Torquay United, Coventry City, Birmingham City and Hereford United where he was also the manager. Signed by Graham Carr during an emergency period, in October 1994. He played just the one game in the BLT tie at Kidderminster, where his solid display at the back helped the team record a 5-1 win. Reappeared in the Conference later the same season with Merthyr Tydfil.

Debut (League Cup) v Kidderminster Harriers (a) 31:10:94

Appearances: 1   League 0   **Goals:** 0
Cups   1

DUDFIELD LAWRIE. Forward. Born Bermondsey. A prolific striker for the Kettering Town youth team during the 1995-96 season winning league and cup double. Became an apprentice at the start of the following season making his Conference debut as a substitute, just 16 years old, during Steve Berry's caretaker player/manager spell at the club. He made his first start against Farnborough Town in the Spalding Challenge Cup. Lawrie rejected new terms with the Poppies opting to join Premiership side Leicester City on professional forms during the 1997-98 close season.

GM Vauxhall Conference, debut v Gateshead (h) 02:11:96

Appearances: 15   League 3+10   **Goals:** 0
Cups   2

DUGGAN DEREK. Midfield. Born Birmingham. Previous clubs: Aston Villa (junior) and Birmingham City. A dynamic player signed by Colin Clarke, joining Kettering in August 1980 from Birmingham. Bagged his first goal for the club in the 2-1 home win against Telford United. Played in a variety of positions, right-back, midfield, centre-forward and on the wing. Scored the final goal of the disastrous 1982-83 campaign, the Poppies losing the vital last game 1-2 at Trowbridge Town. Played just one more game for the Poppies, his final appearance was the 1983-84 opening day home 2-3 defeat by Scarborough. Later played for Nuneaton Borough, Worcester City, Gloucester City and Aylesbury United.

Alliance Premier League, debut v Gravesend & Northfleet (a) 04:10:80

Appearances: 134   League 98+5   **Goals:** 17 League 13
Cups   29   Cups   4

DUNPHY SHAUN*. Centre-back. Born Maltby. Previous clubs: Barnsley, Lincoln City, Doncaster Rovers and Scarborough. Joined the club during the 1994-95 season from Lincoln City, making his debut in the 0-2 defeat at Bath and was never seen again in Kettering's colours, although he did play in the Conference with Halifax Town a little while later.

GM Vauxhall Conference, debut v Bath City (a) 04:02:95

Appearances: 1   League 1   **Goals:** 0
Cups   0

E

EASTHALL FREDDIE. Utility. He played as a winger, in midfield, striker and at full back, whilst in Kettering's colours. Previous club: Kings Lynn. Made his debut for the club in the Southern Premier League, made his Alliance debut against Stafford Rangers, the first ever league game. Scored his first Premier goal against Weymouth in the 3-1 win at Rockingham Road. One Year and five days later he bagged his second goal against AP Leamington again at Rockingham Road. Freddie's final Poppies appearance came during the 1980-81 season a 2-1 home win against Telford United.

Southern Premier League debut v Atherstone (h) 18:10:78
Alliance Premier League, debut v Stafford Rangers (a) 18:08:79

Appearances: 68   League 51+3   **Goals:** 3   League 3
Cups   14

EDWARDS MATTHEW. Winger. Born Hammersmith. Previous clubs: Tottenham Hotspur, Reading and Brighton Hove Albion. Signed by Graham Carr during the 1994-95 close season, but a crucial ligament injury in the pre-season friendlies put him out of action for the whole of that season. Made his Poppies debut in December 1995 as a full back. Left the club later in 1995 and joined Walton & Hersham.

GM Vauxhall Conference, debut v Dover Athletic (a) 02:12:95

Appearances: 4   League 2   **Goals:** 0
Cups   1+1

EDWARDS NEIL. Winger. Born Rowley Regis. Previous clubs: Old Swinford, Wolverhampton Wanderers and Telford United. Joined the Poppies from Wolves during the 1987-88 season. Neil, I feel, was never given enough time to settle in the team and after 'in and out' appearances, he left the Poppies and joined Corby Town in March 1990 and later played for Rothwell Town.

Appearances: 62   League 28+18   **Goals:** 11 League 8
                  Cups   9+7   Cups 3

ELLIS NEIL. Winger. Born Bebington. Previous clubs: Bangor City, Chester City, Maidstone United and Corby Town. Signed during the 1992-93 season by Graham Carr after the demise of Maidstone. Made his only Conference appearance as a substitute in the 1-3 home defeat by Merthyr Tydfil. Neil followed that up with an appearance in the BLT at Kidderminster Harriers - witnessed by 14 Kettering fans in a gate of 624.

GM Vauxhall Conference, debut v Merthyr Tydfil (h) 17:10:92
Appearances: 2   League 0+1   **Goals:** 0
                  Cups 1

EMMS MICKY. A reserve player who stepped up to the first team during Alan Buckley's reign. Made his debut during the 1987-88 season in the FA Trophy 2nd round as a substitute. Made his only other appearance in the 4-0 away win against Wellingborough Town in the Northants Senior Cup semi-final.

Debut (FA Trophy) v Altrincham (h) 04:02:88
Appearances: 2   League 0 **Goals:** 0
                  Cups 0+2

EMSON PAUL. Winger. Born Lincoln. Previous clubs: Darlington, Wrexham, Grimsby Town, Derby County and Brigg Town. Paul, was signed by Peter Morris during the 1990-91 season from Darlington, who won the Vauxhall Conference the previous season. Emson, a feature of that side, scored on his debut for the Poppies against Welling in the 1-0 BLT win at Rockingham Road. Never a consistent member of the team he left the following season and briefly joined Gateshead.

Debut (League Cup) v Welling United (h) 07:03:91
GM Vauxhall Conference, debut v Merthyr Tydfil (a) 09:03:91
Appearances: 19   League 13+3   **Goals:** 3 League 2
                  Cups 2+1   Cups 1

ENGLAND. Nine players have represented the England semi-professional team since 1979 whilst playing for the Poppies. The full list is as follows.

England Caps: **Brendan Phillips**, 1980 - S (*), H = 2 caps. **Robbie Cooke**, 1989 - W(*),1990 - I (*) = 2 caps. **Paul Nicol**, 1991 - I, W = 3 caps. **Paul Bancroft**, 1991 - W = 1 cap. **Graham Benstead**, 1994 - W, FU21, NU21(*) = 3 caps. **Steve Holden**, 1994 - W, FU21, NU21(*), 1995- H, G = 5 caps. **Nick Ashby**, 1994 - FU21, NU21, 1995 - G = 3 caps. **Ian Arnold**, 1995 - W (*),   H, = 2 caps. **Carl Alford**, 1996 - R = 1 cap.

*Key: FU21   Finland U21, G = Gibralter, H = Holland, I = Italy, NU21 = Norway U21, R = Republic of Ireland, S = Scotland, W = Wales.   * = Appeared as a substitute.*

Carl Alford's 6th minute goal against the Republic of Ireland at Kidderminster Harriers on the 27th February 1996, was the first goal scored by a Kettering player for the National side.   England went on to win 4-0.

EVANS NICKY.

Striker. Born Bedford. Previous clubs: Queens Park Rangers and Peterborough United. 'The Blond Bomber', joined the Poppies from Peterborough in the 1978 close season. Nicky was the second player to score in the Alliance Premier League during the 2-2 draw with Nuneaton Borough in September 1979.   He holds the distinction as the player
who has scored the most goals in a first class game for the Poppies, hitting four against Nuneaton Borough during the 5-1 away win at the Manor Ground in 1981.   During that same season he banged in 7 goals in four games the best of any Poppies striker in recent years.   A prolific goalscorer he netted 29 goals during the 1980-81 season.   He was almost forced to leave the Poppies after finding out he wasn't on the retained list, much to the dismay of all the fans.   Nicky later became a success with Barnet who paid

£2,000 for his services during the 1983-84 close season. Later he moved to Wycombe Wanderers.

Southern Premier League, debut v Margate (a) 26:08:78
Alliance Premier League, debut v Stafford Rangers (a) 18:08:79

Appearances: 147   League 120+1   **Goals:** 62 League 49
Cups   25+1   Cups   13

EVER PRESENT. The following 16 players have played in every league game during a season, for the record:

Peter Phipps (38*, 1* as a substitute) and Sean Suddards (38 in 1979-80),

Peter Phipps, Sean Suddards and Peter Walters (38 in 1980-81),

Frankie Murphy (42 in 1982-83),

Dave Wharton (42 in 1984-85),

Tim Thacker (42 in 1985-86),

Arthur Mann (42 in 1986-87),

Mark Smith (42 in 1987-88),

Mark Nightingale (40 in 1988-89),

Paul Nicol (42 in 1990-91),

Richard Hill (42*, 1* as a substitute) and Richard Huxford (42 in 1991-92),

Phil Brown (42* in 1992-93, *2 as a substitute),

Nick Ashby (42 in 1993-94).

F

FA CUP. Kettering have enjoyed a fair amount of success during the 19 seasons covered by this book. Since 1979 the club has reached the First Round proper on 13 occasions, the 2nd Round on 3 occasions, the 3rd Round on 2 occasions and the 4th Round once. The highest attendance involving the Poppies was 16,001 for the 4th Round game against Charlton Athletic at Selhurst Park. The highest home attendance was 6,100 for the local derby 1st Round tie against Northampton Town. Robbie Cooke scored 11 goals during the 1988-89 campaign - the highest tally in the complete competition that season, while Phil Brown scored in five consecutive matches during a two season period.

FANZINE. Kettering Town FC have one unofficial publication called PATGOD, (Poppies At The Gates Of Dawn). Run by a group of fans for the fans. To my knowledge the publication has been banned by the Football Club on at least three occasions.

FATHER & SON. The only father and son combination to play for the Poppies since 1979 are Roger and Nick Ashby - both full backs. Although Roger holds the club record all time appearances, son Nick played in the Conference for Kettering more times than his father.

Manager Steve Berry's first appointment during the 1996-97 season was John Gaunt father of central defender Craig, as his assistant. John a former Derby County and Nottingham Forest player also spent 12 years at Notts County as reserve/youth team coach.

Striker Tony Loughlan who played during the opening 1993-94 season matches is the son of John Loughlan who played for the club during the 1970's in the Southern Premier League.

FA TROPHY. The Competition was well under way when the Alliance Premier League was formed, having been initialised for the onset of the 1969-70 season. In 1979-80 the Poppies met Merthyr Tydfil at Pennydarren Park and suffered a 1st Round 3-0 defeat. Trophy success has so far alluded Kettering Town, with only one Wembley appearance to their credit (1978-79) and a semi-final showdown against Runcorn in 1985-86. The Linnets winning 2-0 at Rockingham Road taking the aggregate score by the same margin. In more recent years the Trophy - now sponsored by Umbro - has become a bit of an 'Achilles Heel' as the likes of Chelmsford City, Billingham Synthonia, Boreham Wood, Emley, Marine, etc have knocked the club out of the competition at an alarming rate. The largest home attendance is 4,421 against Woking in 1990-91 - the Poppies winning 2-0 with two Jon Graham goals.

FEE GREG. Central defender. Born Halifax. Joined the Poppies from Bradford City during the 1984-85 close season. While on Kettering's books Greg was a student at Loughborough University and played for the student team that toured Japan in early 1985. A big powerful player who always commanded the heart of the defence, chipped in with the odd goal now and again. The ever popular Fee left Kettering for Boston United during September 1986, much to the annoyance of the fans. Having spoken to Greg at the time, he felt a move was the best way to guarantee a game!

Debut (Maunsell Cup) v Peterborough United (h) 15:08:84
GM Vauxhall Conference, debut v Altrincham (a) 18:08:84

Appearances: 103   League 75+2   **Goals:** 10   League 6
Cups   26   Cups   4

FELTON GRAHAM.   Winger. Born Cambridge. Previous clubs: Cambridge United, Northampton Town and Barnsley. Joined the Poppies in 1977 having represented England at youth level. The majority of Graham's appearances were in the Southern Premier League. Played just the one season in the Alliance making his final appearance in the 1-1 home draw against Nuneaton Borough as a substitute. Left the Poppies for Bedford during the 1980-81 close season.

Southern Premier League, debut v AP Leamington (a) 27:08:77
Alliance Premier League, debut v Stafford Rangers (a) 18.08:79

Appearances: 17   League 13+2   **Goals:** 0
Cups   0+2

FINALS. The Poppies have appeared in three League Cup Finals, winning just one.

Line-ups:

1980-81. Alliance Premier League Cup

v Altrincham (a) First leg, 0-2.

Walters, Curtis, Suddards, Clarke, Forster, Duggan, Guy, Flannagan*, Atkins, Evans, Phipps. Sub, Hofbauer*.

v Altrincham (h) Second leg 2-1.

Walters, Curtis, Suddards, Clarke, Forster, Duggan*, Haverson, Phipps, Hofbauer, Atkins (1), Evans. Sub, Guy* (1).

1986-87. General Motors Acceptance Corporation Cup

v Hendon (h) 3-1.

Harrison, Ward, Mann, Cavener, Lewis, Wood, Keast (1), Richardson, Kellock (1), Smith (1), Daley. Subs unused, Crawley, Birch.

1994-95. Bob Lord Trophy

v Bromsgrove Rovers (a) First leg, 1-4.

Gleasure, Brown, Ashby, Holden, Saddington, Donald*, Price, Chard, Alford, Stringfellow+, Arnold. Subs, Wright+, Clarke* (1).

v Bromsgrove Rovers (h) Second leg, 1-6.

Gleasure, Price, Ashby, Chard, Saddington*, Clarke, Wright, Thomas, Alford (1 pen), Brown, Arnold. Subs, Stringfellow*, Graham.

FIRST GAME. The first game the Poppies contested in the Alliance Premier League was against Stafford Rangers on August 18th at Marston Road, 3 months after Rangers had beaten Kettering 2-0 at Wembley Stadium in the 1979 FA Trophy Final. The League encounter ended 0-0 watched by 2,104. The Kettering Town line up that day was: 1. Lane, 2. Ashby, 3. Hughes, 4. Easthall, 5. Suddards, 6. Clarke, 7. Felton, 8. Evans, 9. Phipps, 10. Clayton, 11. Flannagan, 12. Newman.

FLANNAGAN JOHN. Midfield. Previous clubs: Leicester City, AP Leamington, Atherstone, Nuneaton Borough and Boston United. A fabulous servant to the club with so many impressive performances under his belt and although 'Flannie' played 90 games for the Poppies in the Alliance, the majority of his appearances were made in the Southern Premier League. He scored his first Alliance goal against AP Leamington in the 1-1 home draw and his last the same season in the 1-0 away win at Redditch United. Left the Poppies for Worcester City during the summer of 1981. Later played for Corby Town.

Southern Premier League, debut v Redditch United (a) 01:04:78
Alliance Premier League, debut v Stafford Rangers (a) 18:08:79

Appearances: 93   League 67+1   **Goals:** 4   League 4
                        Cups   19+2

FLATTS MARK. Midfield. Born Haringey. Previous clubs: Grimsby Town, Bristol City, Brighton Hove Albion, Cambridge United (all loans), Torino (Italy) and Arsenal. Originally a trainee with Arsenal. After 16 first team appearances for the Gunners he was released during the 1996-97 close season. Played against the Poppies for Arsenal during the 1995-96 pre-season friendlies. A Steve Berry signing during the 1996-97 season who did not impress and was released after just two appearances (both defeats).

GM Vauxhall Conference, debut v Kidderminster Harriers (a) 14:12:96

Appearances: 2   League 2   **Goals:** 0
                       Cups   0

FLINN GARY. Midfield. Youth team player who made his debut for the club as a substitute during the 5-0 drubbing by Rothwell Town in the 1995-96 Northants Senior Cup semi-final.

Debut (County Cup) v Rothwll Town (a) 27:02:96

Appearances: 1   League 0   **Goals:** 0
                       Cups   0+1

FORSTER MARYTN. Full Back. Born Kettering. Former Nottingham Forest (junior), England schoolboy international. A solid reliable defender with style and class. He left the Poppies for Northampton Town during the 1983-84 close season period. Scored his only Alliance goal in the 2-1 away victory at the Huish, Yeovil - his 5th game for the club.

Debut (FA Trophy) v Gravesend & Northfleet (a) 10:01:81
Alliance Premier League, debut v AP Leamington (h) 21:02:81

Appearances: 92   League 73+1   **Goals:** 1   League 1
                        Cups   17+1

FOSTER BARRY*. A Jim Conde loan signing from Boston United, a full back formerly with Mansfield Town. Joined the Poppies in January 1983 making his debut in the Poppies 4-1 win at Frickley.

Alliance Premier League, debut v Frickley Athletic (h) 22:01:83
Appearances: 5   League 4+1   **Goals:** 0
                Cups   0

FOWLER JOHN. Midfield. Born Preston. Previous clubs: Cambridge United, Preston North End and Cambridge City. A Gary Johnson signing in January 1996, who had played for United in the Second and Third Divisions of the Football League before a loan spell with Cambridge City. Failing to establish himself in a mediocre team John was released at the end of the 1995-96 season.

GM Vauxhall Conference, debut v Dover Athletic (h) 13:01:96
Appearances: 23   League 16   **Goals:** 0
                Cups   7

FOX KEVIN. Goalkeeper. Born Sheffield. Previous clubs: Boston United, Hull City and Lincoln City. Joined the Poppies on free transfer from Lincoln during the summer of 1981 as a replacement for Peter Walters who moved to Scarborough. Kevin left the Poppies for Rushden Town in January 1982 after failing to establish himself.

Alliance Premier League, debut v Maidstone United (h) 15:08:81
Appearances: 15   League 12
                Cups   3

FUCCILLO (Pasqualle) LIL. Full-back. Born Bedford. Previous clubs: Luton Town, Tulsa Roughnecks (USA), Southend United, Peterborough United, a period in Malta and Cambridge United. Peter Morris brought Lil from Cambridge during the 1988-89 close season and what an inspirational signing - a touch of class. One of the best dead ball kickers and penalty takers to have graced Rockingham Road, a superb Captain, a leader on the field. It came as quite a shock and there was sheer disappointment in the town when he left and joined Wivenhoe Town during the 1989-90 close season.

Debut (Maunsell Cup) v Peterborough United (h) 13:08:88
GM Vauxhall Conference, debut v Northwich Victoria (h) 20:06:88
Appearances: 52   League 37+1   **Goals:** 9   League 7
                Cups   13+1   Cups   2

G

GALLAGHER JACKIE*. Striker Previous club: Wolverhampton Wanderers. An inspired signing by Peter Morris towards the end of the 1988-89 campaign. Jackie's last minute winning goal against Kidderminster Harriers sent the majority of the 4,377 fans at Rockingham Road wild as promotion was still in the club's grasp. Sadly, not to be. Jackie later played for Boston United.

Debut (County Cup) v Brackley Town (a) 07:04:89
GM Vauxhall Conference, debut v Fisher Athletic (h) 11:03:89

Appearances: 10   League 8+1   **Goals:** 2   League 2
Cups   1

GAUNT CRAIG. Defender. Born Nottingham. Previous clubs: Bromsgrove Rovers, Scarborough, Chesterfield, Huddersfield Town and Arsenal. Originally a trainee at Arsenal, Craig was signed by Gary Johnson during the 1996-97 close season for £6,000 from Bromsgrove Rovers. An impressive first season with the club, Craig scored his first goal for the Poppies in the away defeat at Morecambe. As the financial situation deepened the club put the entire squad up for sale during the troubled 1997-98 season. Craig's contract was terminated in October 1997, allowing the player to pursue a new career. Joined Ilkeston Town after leaving the Poppies.

GM Vauxhall Conference, debut v Macclesfield Town (a) 17:08:96

Appearances: 45   League 36   **Goals:** 2   League 2
Cups   9

GAVIN PAT*. Striker. Born Hammersmith. Previous clubs: Leicester City, Gillingham and Peterborough United. Signed by Peter Morris during the 1991-92 season. Scored on his debut in the 3-2 win at Welling United. Made a brief return under Graham Carr the following season before joining Farnborough Town.

Appearances: 19   League 18   ***Goals:*** 4   League 4
                 Cups   1

GENERAL MOTORS ACCEPTANCE CORPORATION CUP.

A two season sponsorship taking over from the Bob Lord Trophy in 1986. In the first season the Poppies won the competition beating Hendon 3-1 in front of 1,809 at Rockingham Road, the goals were scored by Billy Kellock, Dougie Keast and Mark Smith. The following season, as holders, the Poppies went out at the 3rd round stage to Northwich Victoria 2-3 in front of 661 at Rockingham Road.

GENERAL MOTORS VAUXHALL CONFERENCE.

The GMVC took over sponsorship from Gola for season 1986-87, and to date is the longest major sponsor of a Professional Football League in the Country. With the new sponsors came automatic promotion (or so it seemed) - the ballot box was dead - Scarborough won the first GMVC title and joined Division 4 - the Poppies finished in 16th place. Since then Maidstone United, Barnet, Wycombe Wanderers and Macclesfield Town are the only other non-league clubs fortunate enough to win the league and take their place in the Football League; as ground regulations etc, have thwarted Conference Champions such as Kiddernminster Harriers, Macclesfield Town (previously in 1994-95) and Stevenage Borough. I have not included Lincoln City, Darlington, Colchester United and Halifax Town as non-league teams as they were league teams relegated and promoted back. Newport County were expelled from the Conference after failing to fulfil a match during the 1988-89 season while Maidstone United folded after three seasons in the Football League. Relegated Football League side Hereford United entered the fray after being relegated from Nationwide Division Three at the end of the 1996-97 season, while Doncaster Rovers were the latest to drop out of the professional circuit a season later. Vauxhall announced that the 1997-98 season would be their last as the Conference's major sponsor and at the time of writing, May 1998, the new sponsors had not been declared.

GENOVESE DOMINIC.

Forward. Born Peterborough. Previous clubs: Stamford AFC, Boston United (twice), Nuneaton Borough, Grantham, Cambridge City, Peterborough United and Grebbestadd (Sweden). Dominic was a member of the Stamford side that reached the 1984 FA Vase final, but was on the losing side. Originally joined the Poppies in August 1986 - a Dave Needham signing but was released by Alan Buckley. Peter Morris brought Dominic back to the Poppies during 1989-90. Later became the Football in the Community Officer for Kettering Town.

GM Vauxhall Conference, debut v Weymouth (a) 16:08:86

Appearances: 35   League 18+9   **Goals:** 10   League 5
                   Cups   4+4   Cups   5

GERNON IRVIN. Full back. Born Birmingham. Previous clubs: Ipswich Town, Gillingham, Reading, and Northampton Town. A Dave Cusack signing from the Cobblers in the summer of 1992. A former England youth and under-21 international. After leaving the Poppies Irvin joined Telford United for a short spell.

Debut (Maunsell Cup) v Peterborough United (h) 08:08:92
GM Vauxhall Conference, debut v Slough Town (a) 22:08:92

Appearances: 39   League 31+1   **Goals:** 0
                   Cups   7

GIANT KILLING. Three Football League clubs have been conquered in the FA Cup since the formation of the Alliance Premier League and two of those, Bristol Rovers and Halifax Town, were dismissed in the same season (1988-89). Maidstone United, then of Division 4, succumbed in 1990-91. Bristol Rovers were beaten 2-1 at Rockingham Road with two goals from Robbie Cooke. The Bristol Rovers manager at that time was the former Tottenham Hotspur boss Gerry Francis and in goal for the Pirates - Leeds United and England's Nigel Martyn. Halifax Town were taken to a replay at the Shay after a 1-1 draw at Kettering, courtesy of a Cohen Griffith goal. The replay was won 3-2 by the Poppies with goals from Russell Lewis and another brace from Cooke. Maidstone United were beaten 2-1 at Watling Street (Dartford) with goals from Phil Brown and an own goal. Since then Halifax Town have been relegated to the Conference and returned as champions to league football. The team coach of Maidstone United was Clive Walker (Graham Carr's assistant at Kettering) and as all Poppies fans remember Darren Oxbrow (later to play for the Poppies), scored the all important winning own goal for Kettering that set up the Blackburn Rovers tie.

GIANT KILLED! The boot has been on the other foot as this section will show. Some of the Poppies most embarrassing exits to lower divisional sides have occurred in the FA Trophy. They are for the record, Mossley (1980-81), Dulwich Hamlet (1982-83 & 1983-84), Burton Albion (1984-85), Gravesend & Northfleet (1988-89), Wokingham (1989-90), Emley (1990-91), Marine (1991-92), Billingham Synthonia (1993-94), Boreham Wood (1994-95), Chelmsford City (1996-97). In the FA Cup only four teams have had a slice of the Poppies, they are Wisbech Town (1987-88), Chelmsford City (1985-86 & 1990-91), Bedworth United (1996-97) and Hinckley United (1997-98).

GLEASURE PETER. Goalkeeper. Born Luton. Previous clubs: Millwall, Northampton Town and Hitchin. Signed during the 1994-95 season from Hitchin as cover for Graham Benstead. Another one of Graham Carr's ex-Northampton Town 1986 Division 4 Championship winning side to grace the Rockingham Road pitch. Had an extended run in the team after Benstead injured his leg against Woking in the Bob Lord Trophy. Peter was released at the end of the season, joining Nuneaton Borough in the Beazer Midland Division.

Debut (League Cup) v Kidderminster Harriers (a) 31:10:94
GM Vauxhall Conference, debut v Stevenage Borough (h) 26:12:94
Appearances: 26   League 15
Cups   10+1

GOALS. The first goal scored in the Alliance Premier League was by Roy Clayton against Wealdstone at Rockingham Road. In fact Clayton scored both of the goals in the 2-2 draw, witnessed by 2,439. This was the Poppies second match in the newly formed league having drawn the first game 0-0 against Stafford Rangers at Marston Road.
The most goals scored in one league season was 73 in 1994-95. The fewest league goals in a league season, 46 in 1993-94. The fewest league goals conceded, a mere 24 (just 10 away from home, a GMVC record) during 1993-94. The most goals conceded was 99 in 1982-83. Nicky Evans holds the record of goals scored in one match - four against Nuneaton Borough in Kettering's 5-1 away victory during the 1980-81 campaign, while scoring 29 goals in all competitions during the 1980-81 season, the highest total so far.

KETTERING TOWN LEADING LEAGUE SCORERS SINCE 1979

Season	League	Goals	Player
1979-80	APL	12	Roy Clayton
1980-81	APL	21	Nicky Evans
1981-82	APL	16	Frank Murphy
1982-83	APL	23	Frank Murphy
1983-84	APL	14	David Hofbauer
1984-85	GOLA	16	Billy Jeffrey
1985-86	GOLA	11	Ian Crawley
1986-87	GMVC	9	Billy Kellock
	GMVC	9	Mark Smith
1987-88	GMVC	16	Mark Smith
1988-89	GMVC	12	Robbie Cooke
1989-90	GMVC	28	Robbie Cooke
1990-91	GMVC	14	Jon Graham
1991-92	GMVC	17	Jon Graham
1992-93	GMVC	16	Phil Brown
1993-94	GMVC	8	Phil Brown
1994-95	GMVC	23	Carl Alford
1995-96	GMVC	22	Carl Alford
1996-97	GMVC	10	Craig Norman
1997-98	GMVC	14	Chris Pearson

Leading Career Scorers at a glance since 1979:
1. Frank Murphy (82).
2. Phil Brown (68).
3. Nicky Evans (62). Mark Smith (62).
5. Robbie Cooke (60).
6. Carl Alford (54).
7. David Hofbauer (52). Jon Graham (52).
9. Doug Keast (45). Billy Jeffrey (45).

GOALKEEPERS. The Poppies have used 42 different goalkeepers since 1979. The most used in one season was 8 in 1992-93, this could be stretched to 11 if you include the pre-season friendlies and 2 out field players deputising for injured or sent off keepers. Kevin Shoemake holds the most number of appearances since the formation of the Alliance Premier League with 157 (but is way behind Gordon Livsey's all time record of 315 - sorry Kevin).

The list of goalkeepers alphabetically: Fred Barber, Paul Bastock, Andy Beasley, Graham Benstead, Kevin Blackwell, Ian Bowling, Willie Boyd, Jim Brown, Steve Cherry, Steve Conroy, Kevin Fox, Peter Gleasure, Nicky Goodwin, Mark Harrison, Russell Hoult, Gareth Howells, Steve Humphries, Paul Ivey, Alan Judge, Danny Kelly, Frank Lane, Harvey Lim, Mick Martin, John Milkins, Chris Miller, Stuart Naylor, Chris Neville, Paul Pettinger, Andy Poole, Andy Quy, Paul Reece, Peter Ryan, Simon Sheppard, Kevin Shoemake, Mark Smith, Jurgen Sommer, Chris Taylor, Phil Tingay, Neil Torrance, Jason Trinder, Billy Turley, Peter Walters.

Kevin Shoemake went six games during the 1990-91 season without conceding a goal, although he was substituted in the Stafford Rangers home game by Ian Phillips due to an injury. That same season both Shoemake and Paul Bastock kept 17 clean sheets out of the first 23 competitive games of the season, conceding just 14 goals (8 of those in 2 games). 1993-94 saw the club achieve the most clean sheets during a league season when Russell Hoult, and Graham Benstead had 24 shut-outs between them. Hoult conceding just one goal - from a penalty in the eight games he played.

GOALS. The highest aggregate of goals scored in a **league match** is 9. This has occurred three times, only once though in the Poppies favour. For the record:

> 3-6 v Stafford Rangers, 1979-80
> 5-4 v Altrincham, 1981-82
> 2-7 v Barrow, 1981-82

The highest aggregate in a **Cup Competition,** a staggering 12, again not in the Poppies favour. For the record:

> 2-10 v Bromsgrove Rovers, 1994-95 (Bob Lord Trophy
> Final, 2 leg final, 1-4 & 1-6)

GOLA LEAGUE. Season 1984-85 saw the sponsorship of the Alliance Premier League by sports company Gola, and with that came the new title the 'Gola League'. As it turned out Gola only sponsored the league for two seasons. The Poppies finished in 12th and 9th positions. Again like its predecessor, promotion to the Football League was not automatic and relied on the ballot box system. GM Vauxhall, took over from Gola for the onset of the 1986-87 season to form the GMV Conference.

GOODE TERRY. Striker. Born London. Previous club: Birmingham City. Joined the Poppies from Birmingham City in July 1982. Terry scored on his Alliance debut in the 1-1 draw against Trowbridge Town at Rockingham Road. Also had a three goals in a three game spell in January 1983, but was on the losing side twice. Released by Don Masson at the end of the season.

Alliance Premier League, debut v Trowbridge Town (h) 14:08:82

Appearances: 32   League 24+2   **Goals:** 8   League 6
              Cups   6   Cups   2

GOODWIN NICK. Goalkeeper. Born Derby. Originally joined the Poppies from Derbyshire Central Midland League side Graham Street in 1984. Returned to the club after a short spell with Shepshed Charterhouse. Nick finally left Kettering due to frustration of not enough first team football and joined Shepshed in September 1985. Later played for Telford United in the GMVC.

Alliance Premier League, debut v Frickley Athletic (a) 10:04:84

Appearances: 81   League 59
                  Cups   22

GOODWIN MARK. Midfield. Born Sheffield. Previous clubs: Leicester City, Notts County and Walsall. A Peter Morris signing from Walsall during the 1990-91 close season. After considerable league experience with Leicester City, where he won a Second Division Championship medal, and Notts County before his final league port of call Walsall in 1987. After leaving Kettering at the end of 1990-91 season Mark joined Eastwood Town. Scored the first of his five Conference goals against Sutton United at Gander Green in the Poppies 2-1 victory.

Debut (Maunsell Cup) v Peterborough United (h) 14:08:90
GM Vauxhall Conference, debut v Cheltenham Town (h) 21:08:90

Appearances: 43   League 30+3   **Goals:** 5   League 5
              Cups   9+1

GOULD ANDY. Forward. Joined the Poppies during the 1985-86 season from Shepshed. He made his first two Gola League appearances as a substitute against Altrincham and Northwich Victoria.

Gola League, debut v Altrincham (a) 24:08:85

Appearances: 11   League 6+3   **Goals:** 0
              Cups   1+1

GRAHAM JON. Winger. Born Leicester. A winger who on his day could destroy the opponents defence like 'a knife through butter'. In his early days at the club Jon was known as 'Super Sub' as he had the knack of scoring within minutes of coming on. The most notable the brace against Woking in the FA Trophy 1st Round, the weekend after the 'Cards' had beaten West Bromwich Albion 4-2 in the FA Cup. Jon had two spells at the club, originally signing from Leicester United during the 1989-90 season. On leaving the Poppies during the 1992-93 close season, he joined former boss Peter Morris at Boston United for a short time, before a return to the Poppies in 1993-94. Jon's second spell at Rockingham Road was disappointing, he never recaptured his original form and was released by the club at the end of the 1994-95 season, joining Beazer Homes Midland League side Bedworth United. He returned to Rockingham Road with Bedworth who inflicted an embarrassing 1-0, FA Cup 3rd Qualifying Round defeat on the Poppies during the 1996-97 season.

GM Vauxhall Conference, debut v Kidderminster Harriers (a) 16:12:89
Appearances: *170*   League 67+69   ***Goals:*** 52 League 42
                                  Cups   21+13   Cups   10

GREEN PETER. Striker. Previous clubs: Grimsby Town and Kings Lynn. Peter's solitary appearance came in the Northants Senior Cup semi-final defeat at Brackley Town (0-1) during the 1988-89 season.

Debut (County Cup) v Brackley Town (a) 07:03:89
Appearances: 1   League 0   ***Goals:*** 0
                          Cups   0+1

GREEN ROBERT. Goalkeeper. Graduated to first team action due to loanee custodian Steve Conroy being recalled by Rotherham United. Robert made just the one outing against Irthlingborough Diamonds in the Northants Senior Cup sem-final during the 1982-83 season. The Poppies won 4-2.

Debut (County Cup) v Irthlingborough Diamonds (h) 16:03:83
Appearances: 1   League 0
                          Cups   1

GREENWOOD ROGER. Midfield. Born Barnsley. Signed by Dave Cusack during the 1992-93 pre-season after serving his apprenticeship with Hull City. Roger made his one and only league appearance against Telford United in the 1-3 defeat at Bucks head. Released when Graham Carr took over as manager.

GM Vauxhall Conference, debut v Telford United (a) 15:09:92

Appearances: 1   League 1   **Goals:** 0
                      Cups   0

GRIFFITH COHEN. Winger. Born Georgetown. Peter Morris bought Cohen for £4,000 from Leicester United during the 1988-89 close season. A flying winger who came into the Nations front rooms during the 1988-89 FA Cup 3rd Round match against Halifax Town when he scored a brilliant individual goal in front of the BBC Match of the Day cameras. Cohen achieved cult status while with the Poppies, every coloured winger to date has tried to fill his boots since but unfortunately hasn't been able to lace them. A brilliant individual who was missed terribly when he left Kettering for Cardiff City for a £60,000 fee in October 1989.

GM Vauxhall Conference, debut v Northwich Victoria (h) 20:08:88

Appearances: 57   League 37+8   **Goals:** 14 League 11
                      Cups   10+2   Cups   3

Cohen Griffith - 'The Flying Winger'

GUY ALAN. An 1981-82 pre-season signing by Colin Clarke from Peterborough United. Alan only made a few appearances due to injury problems making his Alliance debut on the opening day of the season.

Alliance Premier League, debut v Maidstone United (h) 15:08:81

Appearances: 7   League 6+1   **Goals:** 0
                                    Cups   0

GUY CLINT. Striker. Previous club: Mansfield Town. Joined Kettering during the 1980 summer period from Mansfield Town. Clint had the unenviable task of trying to fill the boots left by the vacated Roy Clayton and although he scored a few memorable goals, taking six games to get off the mark, after one season he joined neighbours Corby Town. Scored both goals in the Poppies 2-2 draw against Bath City at Rockingham Road.

Alliance Premier League, debut v Worcester City (a) 16:08:80

Appearances: 34   League 15+8   **Goals:** 7   League 5
                                    Cups   7+4   Cups   2

GYNN MICHAEL. Experienced midfielder. Born Peterborough. Previous clubs: Peterborough United, Coventry City, Stoke City and Hednesford Town. While with Coventry he won an FA Cup winners medal in 1986. Joined the Poppies during the 1995-96 season after a spell in Malta. Made quite an impression, helping the younger members of Gary Johnson's side through the riggers of the Vauxhall Conference. A class act who still had a lot to offer, with superb vision and play making of the highest quality. Released by the club at the end of the 1995-96 season, joining returning Poppies boss Peter Morris at King's Lynn. Later played for Corby Town.

GM Vauxhall Conference, debut v Farnborough Town (h) 16:12:95

Appearances: 20   League 13   **Goals:** 2   League 0
                                    Cups   7   Cups   2

H

HALLUM LYNDON. Midfield. A 1991-92 signing by Peter Morris from Clipstone Miners Welfare. Lyndon played just one game in the semi-final of the Northants Senior Cup, Poppies winning 1-0.
Debut (County Cup) v Northampton Spencer (h) 04:02:92
Appearances: 1   League 0   **Goals:** 0
Cups   1

HAMILL STEWART. Winger. Born Glasgow. Previous clubs: Leicester City, Isabellas and Scunthorpe United. Stewart scored both of his goals in the away fixtures at Barnet and Bangor City during the 1982-83 season. Left Kettering during the summer of 1983 for Nuneaton Borough, linking up with a later Poppies manager Graham Carr.
Alliance Premier League, debut v Runcorn (a) 05:10:82
Appearances: 35   League 28   **Goals:** 2   League 2
Cups   7

HARDING PAUL*. Midfield. Born Mitcham. Previous clubs: Cardiff City, Birmingham City, Notts County, Southend United, Watford and Barnet. Signed by Gary Johnson on loan from Cardiff. Made six appearances at the beginning of the 1996-97 season before being released.
GM Vauxhall Conference, debut v Macclesfield Town (a) 17:08:96
Appearances: 6   League 4+2   **Goals:** 0
Cups   0

HARMON DARREN. Midfielder. Born Northampton. Previous clubs: Notts County, Shrewsbury Town and Northampton Town. A gritty diminutive midfielder signed by Gary Johnson during the 1995-96 season from Northampton Town. Darren led the sponsors choice of man-of-the-match on five occasions, and was named as the 'Supporters' Player of the Season' as well as a tour place with the Middlesex Wanderers to Vietnam. Darren scored his opening Conference goal from the penalty spot in the 2-3 home defeat by Welling United during the 1996-97 season whilst going onto become the midfield dynamo the team needed through a difficult season. Freed by the club at the end of the season.

GM Vauxhall Conference, debut v Woking (h) 12:09:95

Appearances: 77   League 46+12   **Goals:** 6   League 3
                  Cups   19   Cups   3

HARRIS TERRY. Striker. Previous clubs: Enfield, Sheffield United and Grantham. A Graham Carr signing during the 1992-93 season from Grantham, Terry scored three goals in three successive games, against Woking, Gateshead and Stalybridge Celtic in March/April, recording a loss, draw and win, with his efforts. Joined Bridlington, before their demise.

GM Vauxhall Conference, debut v Merthyr Tydfil (a) 09:03:93

Appearances: 9   League 3+4   **Goals:** 3   League 3
               Cups   2

HARRISON ANDY. Midfield. Previous clubs: Boston United, Burton Albion and Christchurch (New Zealand). Brother of goalkeeper Mark, Andy signed for Kettering in January 1986 making his Gola League debut at Holker Street, Barrow in the Poppies 0-1 defeat. Left the club at the end of the season after making 23 consecutive appearances and joined Scarborough.

Gola League, debut v Barrow (a) 11:01:86

Appearances: 25   League 17   **Goals:** 0
               Cups   8

HARRISON MARK. Goalkeeper. Born Spondon, Derbyshire. Previous clubs: Nottingham Forest, Port Vale, Stoke City and Helenic (South Africa). Joined the Poppies in October 1985 and left for Stafford Rangers, (where later he would have a short spell as manager), during the 1987-88 close season. Has the unfortunate distinction of being the Poppies goalkeeper during the worst league defeat 0-8 v Sutton United in season 1986-87 (but it is not the worst in the club's history) since 1979. Earned a GMACC winners medal with the club in the 3-1 victory over Hendon.

Debut (Maunsell Cup) v Northampton Town (h) 30:10:85
Gola League, debut v Maidstone United (a) 02:11:85

Appearances: 58   League 43
               Cups   15

HAT-TRICKS. Fourteen hat-tricks have been scored by Poppies players since the formation of the Alliance Premier. In order they are:
- David Hofbauer v Frickley Athletic (15:11:80),
- Nicky Evans v Nuneaton Borough (18:04:81),
- Frankie Murphy v Trowbridge (29:09:81),
- Frankie Murphy v Bangor City (25:09:82),
- David Hofbauer v Yeovil Town (30:04:83),
- Mark Smith v Enfield (24:11:84),
- Ian Crawley v Boston United (01:01:86),
- Robbie Cooke v Fisher Athletic (23:09:89),
- Paul Bancroft v Fisher Athletic (22:09:90),
- Jon Graham v Sutton United (01:05:91),
- Ian Arnold v Halifax Town (11:03:95),
- Carl Alford v Bromsgrove Rovers (06:05:95),
- Carl Alford v Altrincham (25:11:95),
- Tony Lynch v Gateshead (02:10:96).

HAVERSON PAUL. Previous clubs: Queens Park Rangers and Wimbledon. Joined the Poppies during the 1979-80 season from Wimbledon for £2,000. A stylish centre back who made his debut in the 0-1 away defeat at Telford United. In the next match away at Barrow he opened his scoring account in the 2-1 Poppies win. The following season, he scored again against Barrow at Holker Street, this time though the Poppies lost 1-2. After making just four appearances during the 1982-83 season, due to injury, he joined Enfield in January 1983.

Alliance Premier League, debut v Telford United (a) 29:12:79

Appearances: 109   League 82+1   **Goals:** 5   League 5
                          Cups   25+1

HAWORTH ROBERT. Born. Edgeware. A towering centre-forward who joined the club from Millwall during the 1995-96 season. Prior to his time with the Lions he was on Fulham's books where he was a trainee. After a brief career with the club he left the Poppies in March 1996 and joined Aylesbury United - scoring on his debut for the Ducks. Later played for St Albans.

GM Vauxhall Conference, debut v Farnborough Town (h) 16:12:95

Appearances: 13   League 8   **Goals:** 2   League 2
                          Cups   3+2

HEFFERNAN LIAM. Forward. Previous club: Chesham United. Made his debut for the side in the 1-0 home win against Gateshead during the 1995-96 season. Liam made 3 appearances for the club before making the short trip to Rockingham Triangle to help out Corby Town. A student who was going on to further his education in the USA, after a short football career.

GM Vauxhall Conference, debut v Gateshead (h) 09:03:96

Appearances: 3   League 2   **Goals:** 0
                Cups   1

HERCOCK DAVID. Forward. Previous clubs: Sheffield Wednesday and Cambridge City. A Steve Berry signing during the 1997-98 close season from Premiership club Sheffield Wednesday. Declining terms with the Owls to pursue a career in football and a course at Nottingham University. After a successful period at the Poppies David was allowed to join Ilkeston Town on a free transfer during September 1997. Later played for Nuneaton Borough.

Debut (Maunsell Cup) v Northampton Town (h) 29:07:97
GM Vauxhall Conference, Debut v Slough Town (h) 16:08:97

Appearances: 11   League 7+2   **Goals:** 0
                Cups   1+1

HEYWOOD DAVID. Full-back. Born Wolverhampton. Previous club: Wolverhampton Wanderers. Joined the Poppies during the 1986-87 season from Wolves, making his debut in the game against Barnet, with former Poppy Keith Alexander scoring the own goal in the 1-1 home draw. Scored two goals for the club, his first in the 2-0 win over Aylesbury United in the GMACC semi-final. David's only Conference goal came the following season in the 2-0 away win at Wealdstone. Left the Poppies for Stafford Rangers.

GM Vauxhall Conference, debut v Barnet (h) 11:03:87

Appearances: 74   League 47+7   **Goals:** 2   League 1
                Cups   21   Cups   1

HICKTON DOUG. Striker. Previous clubs: Telford United, Yeovil Town, Burton Albion and Boston United. Signed by Colin Clarke from Boston United in 1979. Doug scored his only goal on his debut as a substitute against Barnet in the 1-0 home win during the 1979-80 campaign.

Alliance Premier League, debut v Barnet (h) 17:11:79

Appearances: 6   League 3+1   **Goals:** 1   League 1
                Cups   2

HILLSBOROUGH APPEAL FUND. This was a game organised for the appalling tragedy that befell Liverpool fans during the opening minutes of their FA Cup semi-final against Nottingham Forest at Hillsborough, Sheffield, where 96 supporters lost their lives on April 15th, 1989. The Poppies met rivals Corby Town at Rockingham Triangle on April 29th, 1989, beating the Steelmen 5-0 with goals from Robbie Cooke, Roy Boon, Glenn Beech, Ernie Moss and Dougie Keast.

HILL RICHARD. Midfield. Born Hinckley. Previous clubs: Nuneaton Borough, Northampton Town, Watford and Oxford United. A Peter Morris signing during the 1991-92 close season, after his league career had ended due to injury. A stylish midfielder who on his day could turn a game. Both of his goals in the 2-2 draw against Colchester United at Rockingham Road were majestic. Acquired the nickname 'Swampy'. On leaving the Poppies, due to injury, he became Football Community Officer at Reading.

GM Vauxhall Conference, debut v Altrincham (a) 17:09:91

Appearances: 76   League 54+1   **Goals:** 23 League 19
                       Cups   21   Cups   4

HINES STEVE. Full-back. Previous clubs: Nottingham Forest, Grantham, Stamford and Kings Lynn. Signed for the Poppies in November 1985 from Kings Lynn but left for Corby Town during the 1986 summer period after just a season's play. Steve scored his first Gola goal during his third game for the club in the 4-2 home win over Barrow and his final goal against Bath City on December 28th 1985 in the 2-0 win at Rockingham Road.

Debut (Maunsell Cup) v Northampton Town (h) 30:10:85
Gola League, debut v Maidstone United (a) 02:11:85

Appearances: 31   League 22+2   **Goals:** 2 League 2
                       Cups   7

HODGES DAVID. Striker. Born Hereford. Previous clubs: Mansfield Town, Torquay United and Gloucester City. Signed by Graham Carr from Gloucester City during the 1992-93 season, made a spectacular start scoring on his debut against Witton Albion - one of only three Poppies players to score on his debut coming on as a substitute. Acquired the nickname 'Chugger' and became almost a cult hero in his short stay with the club. Joined Worcester City after leaving the Poppies.

GM Vauxhall Conference, debut v Witton Albion (h) 27:02:93

Appearances: 14   League 11+1   *Goals:* 5   League 3
                 Cups   2   Cups   2

HODGSON GARY. Central defender, who made his debut for the club during the 1983-84 season against Nuneaton Borough in the 3-4 defeat at Rockingham Road. He left to play in Sweden during 1984.

Alliance Premier League, debut v Nuneaton Borough (h) 28:01:84
Appearances: 2   League 2   **Goals:** 0
                 Cups   0

HOFBAUER DAVID. Striker. Born Northampton. Previous club: Corby Town. Joined the Poppies in the summer of 1979. David scored the first Poppies hat-trick in the Alliance Premier in November 1980 during the 6-1 home thrashing of Frickley Athletic, he also scored the Poppies last hat-trick in the same competition against Yeovil Town, before Gola's sponsorship of the Alliance. To date he is one of only three Kettering players to have scored two hat-tricks in any first class game since 1979. David would have made many more appearances for the club but for the consistency of Stewart Atkins and Nicky Evans. He went on to have a distinguished career with Corby Town.

Alliance Premier League, debut v Scarborough (h) 09:02:80
Appearances: 142   League 93+20   **Goals:** 52 League 44
                    Goals   24+5   Cups   8

HOLDEN STEPHEN. Central defender. Born Luton. Joined the Poppies originally as a loan player from Carlisle United, a central defender who had two brilliant seasons with the club, one which earned him 'Supporters' Player of the Year' for 1993-94, and earned him the chant 'You'll never beat Steve Holden'. Sadly his third season wasn't up to his normal standards even as club captain and he was released by mutual consent, later joining Rushden & Diamonds. Originally a trainee with Leicester City he signed for the Poppies permanently during the 1993-1994 season. His performances where so impressive he was selected to play for the England semi-professional side and gained 5 caps whilst in Kettering's colours. Later played for Stevenage Borough and Cambridge City.

GM Vauxhall Conference, debut v Southport (h) 20:11:93
Appearances: 107   League 83   **Goals:** 4   League 3
                   Cups   24   Cups   1

HOLLIDAY DEAN. A former product of the youth team Dean made his Poppies debut under Steve Berry's management as a second half substitute in the Spalding Challenge Cup, Kettering won 3-1.

Debut (League Cup) v Dover Athletic (a) 07:10:97
Appearances: 1 League 0   **Goals:** 0
Cups   0+1

HOPE CHRIS*. Central defender. Born Sheffield. Chris made a very good impression during his loan spell from Nottingham Forest during the 1992-93 season. Scored on his debut against Yeovil Town during the 3-0 victory at Rockingham Road. He built a good understanding with Darren Oxbrow and was sadly missed when the club failed to sign him on a permanent basis. He went on to play for Scunthorpe United.

GM Vauxhall Conference, debut v Yeovil Town (h) 12:12:92
Appearances: 23   League 19   *Goals:* 3   League 3
Cups   4

HORWOOD NEIL. Forward. Born Peterhead. Previous clubs: Grantham, Kings Lynn, Grimsby Town, Tranmere Rovers, Cambridge United, Welling United and Spalding United. Joined the Poppies during the 1989-90 close season for a £6,000 fee from Spalding United. A Peter Morris signing who unfortunately will always be remembered for the miss he conjured up in front of goal against Northampton Town in the FA Cup 1st Round match at Rockingham Road in 1989. The Cobblers finally won 1-0. Horwood could have been a hero etched into the history books if his effort had gone in. Left Kettering in 1990 as part of the Andy Hunt swop deal with former club Kings Lynn.

GM Vauxhall Conference, debut v Runcorn (h) 26:08:89
Appearances: 14   League 9+3   *Goals:* 0
Cups   2

HOULT RUSSELL*. Goalkeeper. Born Leicester. Joined the club on loan from Leicester City for the start of the 1993-94 season. Only conceded one goal during his stay and that was a mis-kicked slice double taken fluked controversial penalty - (sorry Telford). Damaged his hand against Macclesfield Town and went back to Leicester. A great goalkeeper in the making - later played for Lincoln City and Derby County.

Debut (Maunsell Cup) v Northampton Town (h) 07:08:93

66

GM Vauxhall Conference, debut v Halifax Town (a) 21:08:93
Appearances: 9   League 7
                     Cups   2

HOWARTH LEE*. Born Bolton. Previous clubs: Chorley, Peterborough United, St Patricks (Ireland) and Boston United. Central defender signed on loan during the 1991-92 season from Peterborough United. Made his Conference debut with the club in the 2-0 win at Slough Town. Returned to Peterborough after his loan period expired.
GM Vauxhall Conference, debut v Slough Town (a) 14:03:92
Appearances: 6   League 6   ***Goals:*** 0
                     Cups   0

HOWE 'BOBBY' STEPHEN*. Midfield. Born Annitsford. A loan signing made by Graham Carr from Nottingham Forest during the 1994-95 season. In the short time he was at the club he did enough to show his stay would be a short one - and it was. Scored his only Conference goal (the winning goal as it turned out) against Stalybridge Celtic in the Poppies 1-0 home win. Also scored the last minute equaliser in the 2-2 FA Trophy tie against Waltham & Hersham, forcing a replay. After a series of impressive displays, Frank Clark, then manager of Nottingham Forest, recalled him.
GM Vauxhall Conference, debut v Altrincham (h) 17:12:94
Appearances: 8   League 6   ***Goals:*** 2   League 1
                     Cups   2   Cups   1

HOWELLS GARETH*. Goalkeeper. Born Guildford. Previous clubs: Torquay United and Farnborough Town. Signed from Farnborough Town by Graham Carr during a Christmas crisis in the 1992-93 period. Within 30 seconds of his debut against Stafford Rangers, the Poppies were a goal down, within 3 minutes 2-1 down and at full time amazingly Kettering won 4-2, the club's first away victory of the season. It was also Gareth's last. Went on to play against Kettering for St Albans in the FA Trophy during the 1995-96 campaign.
GM Vauxhall Conference, debut v Stafford Rangers (a) 19:12:92
Appearances: 1   League 1
                     Cups   0

HUGHES LYNDON. Full Back. Previous clubs: West Bromwich Albion and Peterborough United. Joined the Poppies from

Peterborough. His professional career was ruined after the removal of a kidney. Joined the Poppies from Peterborough during the 1978 close season period. Scored his only goal for Kettering in the Alliance Premier League Cup 4-0 win over AP Leamington. Lyndon joined Bromsgrove Rovers during the 1980-81 close season.

Southern Premier League, debut v Margate (a) 26:08:78
Alliance Premier League, debut v Stafford Rangers (a) 18:08:79

Appearances: 13   League 11   **Goals:** 1   League 0
                Cups 2   Cups 1

HUMPHRIES STEVE. Goalkeeper. Born Hull. Previous clubs: Telford United, Doncaster Rovers, Wrexham, Cardiff City and Oldham. Steve made his original debut and only appearance on loan from Leicester City against Barnet during the 1982-83 season, the Poppies winning 3-0. He joined Kettering the following season, leaving to join Barnet in 1984-85. Steve unfortunately broke his leg playing for the Bees against the Poppies during the 1986-87 season but didn't hold that against the club as 'Humphs' rejoined the Poppies for 12 games during the 1992-93 season. Later rejoined Telford United.

Alliance Premier League, debut v Barnet (h) 03:01:83

Appearances: 65   League 54
                       Cups 11

HUNT ANDY. Striker. Born Thurrock. Previous club: Kings Lynn. Signed by Peter Morris during August 1990 from Kings Lynn. He rose through the Linnets youth and reserve ranks and was spotted by Morris during a friendly. Impressive from the word go, most supporters knew Andy's stay at Rockingham Road would be a short one. After a string of impressive performances he left the Poppies for Newcastle United - for a club record fee of £150,000 - signed by Ossie Ardilles, instigated by Peter

Andy Hunt in the colours of West Bromwich Albion, with James Saddington looking on.

Mallinger (who would later become the Poppies chairman). Scored his first goal for the Poppies at Underhill, Barnet, the Poppies winning 1-0. Barnet went on to win the Championship. Andy went on to play for West Bromwich Albion after his time at Newcastle.

GM Vauxhall Conference, debut v Gateshead (h) 25:08:90

Appearances: 27   League 23+1   ***Goals:*** 6   League 6
               Cups   3

HUNTER JUNIOR.
Full back. Born Lambeth. Became Gary Johnson's first signing during the 1995-96 close season, from former club Cambridge United. Although a forward at Cambridge, he played a full-back role at Kettering. Junior was sent off on his club debut against Rushden & Diamonds in the Northants Senior Cup final. But will be remembered for a brilliant strike when playing as a forward at Runcorn, ala Tony Yeobah's (Leeds United) volley against Liverpool. Never looked comfortable as a full-back and became a bit of a liability in the tackle. Left the Poppies during November 1995 and joined Woking in January 1996 - scoring 4 goals on his debut for the Surrey club.

Debut (County Cup) v Rushden & Diamonds (a) 27:07:95
GM Vauxhall Conference, debut v Runcorn (h) 26:08:95

Appearances: 22   League 15 ***Goals:*** 2   League 2
               Cups   5+2   Cups   0

HUXFORD RICHARD.
Full back. Born Scunthorpe. Previous clubs: Scunthorpe United, Burton Albion, Matlock Town and Gainsborough Trinity. A Peter Morris signing during the 1990-91 close season after the defender had spent three months playing in New Zealand. An attacking dependable full back who oozed class and it was only a matter of time before he left the Poppies, going to Barnet in a 1992 swop deal - Barry Fry, Barnet's manager got the better of the deal. Scored the first of his three goals in the 2-0 home win over Merthyr Tydfil in 1990-91 and his third denying Marc North a hat-trick against Cheltenham Town during the same season - did 'Huxey' really touch the ball? Later played for Millwall, Birmingham City, Bradford City, Peterborough United, Burnley and Dunfermline Athletic.

Debut (Maunsell Cup) v Peterborough United (h) 14:08:90
GM Vauxhall Conference, debut v Bath City (a) 18:08:90

Appearances: 103   League 77+2   ***Goals:*** 3   League 3
               Cups   21+3

Richard Huxford - defender.

I

IBRAHIM MUSTAFA. Central defender signed by Gary Johnson as cover during the 1995-96 season. But found himself in the hub of the action as injuries and suspensions took their toll. Scored his only goal for the club against St Albans in the FA Trophy 1st Round replay, the Poppies going on to win 3-2 after extra time. Mustafa was released during the 1996-97 close season.

GM Vauxhall Conference, debut v Bromsgrove Rovers (h) 21:10:95
Appearances: 18   League 8+3   **Goals:** 1   League 0
Cups 7   Cups 1

INTERNATIONAL MATCHES. There have been three international matches staged at Rockingham Road, since 1979. The England semi-professional team met Italy on Tuesday March 5th 1991, the match was drawn 0-0 and featured Kettering's Paul Nicol. England's Under 18 side met Sweden in the UEFA Championship on Saturday 18th November 1995, this match was won 5-2 by England and featured Leicester City's rising talent, Emile Heskey. England's Under 16 side met Croatia in the UEFA Championship on Thursday 5th March 1998, the match ending in a 1-1 draw

IVEY PAUL. A forward, signed by Jim Conde in December 1982, having played previously in the Swedish 1st Division. The former Birmingham City player found himself in goal - due to an injury crisis against Barking in the FA Trophy replay. He did well and the tie went to a third replay after the second one ended 0-0 - the Poppies finally winning 2-0.

Alliance Premier League, debut v Barrow (h) 04:12:82
Appearances: 3   League 2   **Goals:** 0
Cups 1

J

JAMES MICKY. Signed from Sutton Coldfield during the 1986-87 season. Made his debut for the Poppies in the Northants Hillier Senior Cup. After just two substitute appearances in the league Micky joined Hednesford Town.

Debut (County Cup) v Corby Town (a) 13:04:87
GM Vauxhall Conference, debut v Telford United (a) 03:02:87

Appearances: 3   League 0+2   **Goals:** 0
Cups   1

JEFFREY BILLY. Midfield. Born Helensburgh. Previous clubs: Northampton Town, Oxford United (where he spent 10 seasons) and Blackpool. A Dave Needham signing Billy joined the Poppies from the Cobblers in the summer of 1984. Later he became joint caretaker manager of the club along with Arthur Mann when Needham resigned. He left the club after injury problems, for the sun and warmth of Australia in 1987. While with the Poppies Billy became one of the best goalscorers from midfield the club has ever seen, (many from the penalty spot), and all this achieved during an unpleasant period in the clubs history. Billy was the Poppies leading league scorer during the 1985-86 season with 16 Gola goals. Later joined Roger Ashby as his assistant at Rushden & Diamonds.

Debut (Maunsell Cup) v Peterborough United (h) 15:08:84
Gola League, debut v Altrincham (a) 18:08:84

Appearances: 137   League 100+2 **Goals:** 45 League 31
Cups   35   Cups   15

JENAS DENNIS. Forward. Born Nottingham. Previous clubs: Shepshed Charterhouse, Matlock, Burton Albion, Grantham and Nuneaton Borough. A 1984-85 pre-season signing from Shepshed. Although he only lasted one season and had many doubters, he did

72

score two of his eight goals early on in his Poppies career against Runcorn. Joined Arnold Town after leaving the Poppies.

Debut (Maunsell Cup) v Peterborough United (h) 15:08:84
Gola League, debut v Altrincham (a) 18:08:84

Appearances: 35   League 21+5   ***Goals:*** 8   League 7
                 Cups   7+2   Cups 1

JENKINS IORI. Defender. Born Pontrhydyfen, South Wales. Previous clubs: Chelsea and Brentford. Represented Wales at schoolboy and youth international level. Iori joined the Poppies during the 1981-82 pre-season from the Bees making his debut in the 2-2 draw against Maidstone United on the opening Saturday of the season, but left during the 1982-83 close season. Oddly he rejoined the club again in August 1983, but left for Corby Town in 1984.

Alliance Premier League, debut v Maidstone United (h) 15:08:81

Appearances: 61   League 48+2   ***Goals:*** 0
                 Cups   11

JONES DAVID. Striker. Previous clubs: Reading (apprentice), Chester City and Stockport County. A fireman in the RAF, David signed just before transfer deadline day during the 1995-96 season and left just before the end of the season to take over as the player-manager of VS Rugby.

Debut (League Cup) v Bromsgrove Rovers (h) 03:04:96
GM Vauxhall Conference, debut v Dagenham & Redbridge (a) 06:04:96

Appearances: 2   League 0+1   ***Goals:*** 0
                 Cups   1

JONES GARY. Striker. Born Huddersfield. Previous clubs: Rossington Main, Doncaster Rovers and Grantham. A Peter Morris signing for £17,500 - a then club record fee - from Grantham during January 1990. Although Gary was with the club for two and a half seasons he signed at a time when Robbie Cooke, Ernie Moss and the emerging Andy Hunt were at their prime. Chances were few and far between - the writing was on the wall virtually the day after he scored two stunning goals against Sutton United in 1991, the last match of the season. He was sold for £3,000 to Boston United. Later went on to play for Southend United and Notts County.

GM Vauxhall Conference, debut v Runcorn (a) 27:01:90

Appearances: 48   League 31+7   ***Goals:*** 9   League 4
                 Cups   6+4   Cups 5

JONES JOHN. Midfield. Previous club: Redditch United. Made his Alliance debut against Wealdstone at Rockingham Road in the second game of the 1979-80 season. He scored his opening goal for the Poppies in the 3-6 defeat by Stafford Rangers, scoring two more against Yeovil Town in March 1980 as the Poppies ran out 5-3 winners. John left Kettering during the 1980-81 close season for Telford United.

Alliance Premier League, debut v Wealdstone (h) 22:08:79

Appearances: 35   League 26+3   **Goals:** 4   League 4
Cups   5+1

JONES PAUL. Midfield. Born Walsall. Previous clubs: Wolverhampton Wanderers, Walsall and Wrexham. A Peter Morris signing from Wolves during the 1991-92 season. Paul made his debut for the club on the opening day of the season in the 1-1 draw at Moss Lane, Altrincham. Will be remembered for scoring the second goal of the night having come on for Trevor Christie, in the FA Cup 4th Qualifying Round replay at Marston Road, Stafford - the Poppies winning 2-0, going on to to play Maidstone United. After leaving Kettering, Paul played for Stafford Rangers, returning to Rockingham Road in the colours of his new team.

GM Vauxhall Conference, debut v Altrincham (a) 01:08:91

Appearances: 30   League 15+3   **Goals:** 2   League 0
Cups   9+3   Cups   2

JOHNSON GARY. A former Cambridge United manager, Gary took over the Poppies hot seat in the wake of Graham Carr's departure at the end of the 1994-95 season. Formerly a midfielder at Watford, he spent some years playing in the Swedish Second Division. A move to Cambridge United, (as youth team manager), under the managership teams of Chris Turner and John Beck followed, and eventually the managers mantle became his. Moved to the Poppies during an interim period having been

released by Cambridge, and having joined the scouting staff at Arsenal. Johnson suffered a disappointing first term at the club after a promising start, with Kettering finishing the 1995-96 season in 16th place, their worst position since 1984. His problems continued into the 1996-97 season with an early exit at the hands of Bedworth United in the FA Cup 3rd Qualifying Round. Continued poor results in the Conference and the lowest gate for almost a decade (766 v Hednesford Town) resulted in the sack by October 1996 - just 3 points off the bottom of the league table.

Honours won: Northants Senior Cup 1995-96.

MANAGERIAL RECORD
May 1995 to Oct 1996

	P	W	D	L	F	A
League	56	16	13	27	85	107
Cups	21	10	5	6	31	28
TOTAL	**77**	**26**	**18**	**33**	**116**	**135**

JUDGE ALAN. Goalkeeper. Born Kingsbury. Previous clubs: Hereford United, Oxford United and Bromsgrove Rovers. The experienced custodian was signed from Bromsgrove Rovers for £3,000 in the close season in 1995. Alan had played for Oxford United - where he won a Milk Cup Final medal against QPR, at Wembley. Made quite an impression during his first season with the club with some outstanding performances in front of a poor and regularly changing defence. Such was his popularity with the away fans he won the Chris Greacy Shield, awarded by the Poppies Travel Club. Alan could not repeat his form of the previous season and duelled with Kevin Shoemake and others before being released by the club at the end of the 1996-97 campaign. Later played for Brackley Town.

Debut (County Cup) v Rushden & Diamonds (a) 29:07:95
GM Vauxhall Conference, debut v Altrincham (a) 19:08:95

Appearances: 67   League 50+2
                        Cups   14+1

K

KABIA JIM. Forward. Born Mansfield. Previous clubs: Derby County, Chesterfield, Boston United, Stafford Rangers and Burton Albion. Joined the Poppies from Burton during the 1985-86 close season. Jim scored on his debut during the Poppies 3-0 victory over Nuneaton Borough and his only cup goal came in the 2-3 FA Trophy 1st Round defeat against Yeovil Town at Rockingham Road. He left the club in January 1987 for Wisbech Town.

Gola League, debut v Nuneaton Borough (a) 31:08:85

Appearances: 59   League 40+2   **Goals:** 7   League 6
Cups   16+1   Cups   1

KEARNS OLLIE. The much travelled forward whose previous clubs, include Banbury United, Reading, Oxford United, Walsall, Hereford United and Wrexham. Even with all this experience and over 120 goals in league football, Ollie's only Conference game for the Poppies was against Bath City on the opening day of the 1990-91 season. He did though get on the score sheet against Kettering for Walsall in the 1982-83 FA Cup 1st Round 3-0 victory at Fellows Park, a future Kettering Town manager also scored that day - Alan Buckley.

Debut (Maunsell Cup) v Peterborough United (h) 14:08:90
GM Vauxhall Conference, debut v Bath City (a) 18:08:90

Appearances: 2   League 1   **Goals:** 0
Cups   1

KEAST DOUG. Born Edinburgh. Previous clubs: Hibernian and Shepshed Charterhouse. Joined Kettering from Shepshed in December 1983, scoring on his debut against Weymouth in the 1-1 draw at the Wessex Stadium. One of the great ambassadors of the game and the current leading appearance holder since 1979. He was a player who gave 110% in any position he was picked to play. Dougie left Kettering during the 1985-86 pre-season when he thought the club was going under and joined Nuneaton Borough, but as soon as he heard the club had been saved he rejoined the Poppies, later though in similar circumstances during the 1992-93 close season he joined neighbours Corby Town. That same season he returned to Rockingham Road with the Steelmen in the FA Cup 4th Qualifying tie, a pulsating game the Poppies won 2-1. Dougie was awarded two benefit matches during the 1988-89 season for his services to the club. Ron Atkinson brought Sheffield Wednesday to Rockingham Road, while a match against a 'Kettering Past' side was also arranged. He went on to play for Rushden & Diamonds, Burton Albion and Rothwell Town.

Alliance Premier League, debut v Weymouth (a) 31:12:83

Appearances: 373   League 263+34   **Goals:** 45   League 37
Cups   73+3   Cups   8

Doug Keast - the Poppies leading appearance holder since 1979.

KELLOCK BILLY. Born Glasgow. Billy originally joined the Poppies in 1976 after a Football League career with Aston Villa, Cardiff City, Norwich City and Chelmsford City. Joined the Poppies from Chelmsford City but left Kettering in 1979 without playing a game in the newly formed Alliance for a £25,000 move to Peterborough United - he also made Football League appearances for Luton Town, Wolverhampton Wanderers, Southend United, Port Vale and Halifax Town. He returned to Rockingham Road in July 1986 scoring on his home debut in the 2-0 win over Bath City and one of his cup goals was the opener in the Poppies 3-1 GMACC victory over Hendon. He left the Poppies in February 1988 to work abroad.

Southern Premier League, debut v Margate (h) 28:02:76
GM Vauxhall Conference, debut v Weymouth (a) 16:08:86

Appearances: 77   League 52+6   **Goals:** 14   League 11
                  Cups   18+1   Cups   3

KELLY DANNY. Goalkeeper. Born Lancaster. Previous club: Notts County. A Gary Johnson signing during the 1996-97 close season. Brought in as cover for Alan Judge and Kevin Shoemake. Made his debut and only game for the club aged just 19 in the Spalding Challenge Cup second round the Poppies lost 0-2. Danny was given a free transfer during March 1997 and joined Cambridge City.

Debut (League Cup) v Farnborough Town (h) 19:11:96

Appearances: 1   League 0
                 Cups   1

KELLY EDDIE. The experienced ex-Arsenal and Leicester City player was Don Masson's first signing during the 1982-83 season. Eddie only lasted into the second half of his debut game for the Poppies v Barnet, suffering an injury, Kettering won 3-2. On leaving Kettering he played for Melton Town and Torquay United.

Alliance Premier League, debut v Barnet (a) 02:04:83

Appearances: 1   League 1   **Goals:** 0
                 Cups   0

KELLY WILLIE. A reserve player who was given a stint in the first team by Don Masson. He later joined Corby Town as chances in the Poppies team became very few and far between. Scored his first goal for the Poppies in the 4-1 home win over Telford United during the 1983- 84 season.

Alliance Premier League, debut v Nuneaton Borough (h) 28:01:84

Appearances: 21   League 17+1   **Goals:** 3   League 3
                 Cups   3

KIBLER NIGEL. Forward. Last ditch attempt by Graham Carr during the FA Trophy Billingham Synthonia 2nd Round replay fiasco in the 1993-94 season. Young Nigel went on as a substitute late in the second half, to try and stop the rot, but like the rest of the team he couldn't. Billingham ran out worthy 3-1 winners.

Debut (FA Trophy) v Billingham Synthonia (a) 28:02:94

Appearances: 1   League 0   **Goals:** 0
                    Cups   0+1

KING EDDIE. Defender. Born Haverhill. Signed as an apprentice from the youth team during the 1995-96 season. Made his debut for the club in the Northants Senior Cup defeat at Rothwell, but went on to make his Conference debut in the 2-1 away win at Dagenham & Redbridge. Eddie, a 17 year old, gained valuable experience towards the end of the season making a handful of league appearances. Made just one appearance as a substitute in the Spalding Challenge Cup the following season before being released by Steve Berry.

Debut (County Cup) v Rothwell Town (a) 27:02:96
GM Vauxhall Conference, debut v Dagenham & Redbridge (a) 06:04:96

Appearances: 10   League 4+3   **Goals:** 0
                    Cups   1+2

KING JEFF. Midfield. Previous clubs: Altrincham and Burton Albion. Signed from Burton Albion during the 1984-85 season by Dave Needham. Made his debut in the Bob Lord Trophy 3rd Round against Altrincham a tie the Poppies lost 1-2.

Debut (League Cup) v Altrincham (h) 20:03:85
Gola League, debut v Dagenham (a) 23:03:85

Appearances: 12   League 9+1   **Goals:** 0
                    Cups   2

KIRK DAVID. Born Bulwell (Nottingham). Previous clubs: Burton Albion and Shepshed Charterhouse. A winger signed by Don Masson from Shepshed during the 1983-84 season. He made his debut for the club as a substitute in the 1-3 away defeat at Boston United. Dave scored his only goal for the Poppies in the 3-4 FA Trophy 3rd Qualifying Round defeat by Dulwich Hamlet.

Alliance Premier League, debut v Boston United (a) 19:10:83

Appearances: 7   League 4+1   **Goals:** 1   League 0
                    Cups   2   Cups   1

L

LANE FRANK. Goalkeeper. Previous clubs: Tranmere Rovers, Liverpool and Notts County. Frank had the distinction of being signed by Liverpool's legendary manager Bill Shankley for £25,000 from Tranmere. Joined the Poppies during the 1977-78 season. Retired from the game during the summer of 1980.

Southern Premier League, debut v Weymouth (h) 11:03:78
Alliance Premier League, debut v Stafford Rangers (a) 18:08:79

Appearances: 27   League 23
                      Cups   4

LAWRENCE LES. Striker. Born Rowley Regis (near Wolverhampton). Previous clubs: Stowbridge, Shrewsbury Town, Telford United, Torquay United, Weymouth, Port Vale, Aldershot, Burnley, Rochdale, Peterborough United and Cambridge United. Les scored on his league debut for the club against Northwich Victoria on the opening day of the 1988-89 season, everybody thought the club had signed a real gem, but they were to be disappointed as poor performances followed and Les was sold to Aylesbury United for £10,000 in November of the same season.

Debut (Maunsell Cup) v Peterborough United (h) 13:08:88
GM Vauxhall Conference, debut v Northwich Victoria (h) 20:08:88

Appearances: 10   League 4+4   **Goals:** 1   League 1
                      Cups   1+1

LECZYMSKI ALEX. Forward. Born Rushden. A former Northampton Town trainee who gained first team experience with Kettering under Steve Berry's relegation haunted 1997-98 campaign, coming on as an 86th minute substitute in the 1-1 draw against Morecambe. Also played for Corby Town.

GM Vauxhall Conference, debut v Morecambe (h) 08:11:97

Appearances: 2   League 0+1   **Goals:** 0
                     Cups: 1

80

LEONARD GARY*. A midfielder signed on loan from Northampton Town by Colin Clarke in 1981. Made his debut against Telford United as a substitute, replacing David Hofbauer - the Poppies lost 1-3. Gary returned to the Cobblers when his loan period came to an end, the Poppies not being able to afford another term.

Alliance Premier League, debut v Telford United (h) 08:09:81
Appearances: 8   League 5+1   **Goals:** 0
                       Cups 2

LEWIS RUSSELL. Central defender. Born Blaengwynfi, Wales. Previous clubs: Bridgend, Swindon Town and Northampton Town. Russell occupied the centre of defence and was a commanding figure having had a vast amount of Football League experience with Swindon and Northampton. One of the classic Kettering defenders, with Lewis in the side one had the feeling of invincibility, he was that good. Russell joined the Poppies in the 1986 close season. He scored his first Conference goal in the 2-0 win at Bucks Head, Telford during the 1986-87 season and his second in the return match at Rockingham Road in April 1986. A colossus who formed a superb defensive partnership with Andy Tillson. It was a blow to all the fans when Russell left the Poppies due to work commitments in Wales and joined Merthyr Tydfil. While with the Poppies, Russell captained the Welsh semi-professional side.   Later became the Football in the Community Officer for Northampton Town.

GM Vauxhall Conference, debut v Weymouth (a) 16:08:86
Appearances: 192   League 150   **Goals:** 11 League 7
                        Cups   42   Cups   4

LIM HARVEY. Goalkeeper. Born Halesworth. Previous clubs: Norwich City, Plymouth Argyle and Gillingham. Harvey became a crowd favourite in the very short time he played for the club. Initially he played on loan from Gillingham in place of the injured Kevin Shoemake - making his best performance in the thrilling 1-2 away defeat at the hands of First Division Charlton Athletic in the FA Cup 4th Round. Towards the end of his loan spell he decided to try his luck playing in Sweden. He made a re-appearance for the Poppies during the 1992-93 season but went on to play football in Hong Kong soon after.

GM Vauxhall Conference, debut v Runcorn (h) 31:12:88
Appearances: 24   League 16
                       Cups   8

LOUGHLAN TONY. Striker. Born Croydon. Previous clubs: Leicester United and Nottingham Forest. Injury ruined a promising career after a debut goal for Forest against Wimbledon after just 56 seconds. Tony signed during the 1993-94 pre-season from Nottingham Forest, but didn't settle and left for trials at Wycombe Wanderers. Later played for Lincoln City, Dundalk and Corby Town. The son of former Poppies full back John who starred in the 1970's. Tony's only Conference goal was in the 2-0 away win at Kidderminster Harriers.

Debut (Maunsell Cup) v Northampton Town (h) 07:08:93
GM Vauxhall Conference, debut v Halifax Town (a) 21:08:93

Appearances: 6   League 5   **Goals:** 2   League 1
                        Cups   0+1   Cups   1

LYNCH TONY. Striker. Born Paddington. Previous clubs: Brentford, Wealdstone, Maidstone United, Barnet, Cheltenham Town, Stevenage Borough, Yeovil Town and Cape Cod Crusaders (USA). Signed by Gary Johnson during the 1996-97 close season. A member of both Barnet and Stevenage Borough, Vauxhall Conference Championship winning sides. A former groundsman (while at Wealdstone), Tony became the 14th Poppy since 1979 to score a hat-trick, he achieved this against Gateshead (4-1) at Rockingham Road, November 2nd, 1996. After an unsettled period at the club Tony moved to Peterborough United towards the latter part of the season.

GM Vauxhall Conference, debut v Macclesfield Town (a) 17:08:96

Appearances: 36   League 24+6   **Goals:** 8   League 7
                        Cups   4+2   Cups   1

LYNE NEIL. Striker. Born Leicester. Previous clubs: Leicester United, Nottingham Forest, Walsall, Shrewsbury Town, Cambridge United, Chesterfield, Hereford United and Northampton Town. Steve Berry's first signing as Kettering Town manager during the 1996-97 campaign. Scored his first goal for the club in the 3-1 home win over Kidderminster Harriers. Although on contract throughout the 1997-98 season he never played for the club again, due to persistent injury.

GM Vauxhall Conference, debut v Slough Town (h) 07:12:96

Appearances: 21   League 19   **Goals:** 3   League 3
                        Cups   2

M

MACKAY ROGER. Defender. Previous clubs: Mansfield Town, Coventry City, Hendon and Sutton United. Joined the Poppies from Sutton during the 1987-88 close season making his debut in the 1-0 home win over Telford United. Left the club during the 1988-89 close season.

GM Vauxhall Conference, debut v Telford United (h) 31:08:87

Appearances: 28   League 19+2   **Goals:** 0
                        Cups   6

MAGEE JON. Striker. Joined the club from Irish side Bangor during the 1994-95 season, while also a college student at Loughborough. Was given little opportunity but did score on his debut away at Kidderminster Harriers during the 5-1 BLT victory.

Debut (League Cup) v Kidderminster Harriers (a) 31:10:94
GM Vauxhall Conference, debut v Runcorn (h) 05:11:94

Appearances: 4   League 0+2   **Goals:** 1   League 0
                      Cups   1+1   Cups   1

MANAGERS. The Poppies have had ten different managers since 1979, although there have been a few caretakers during interim periods:
- Colin Clarke 1979-82,
- Jim Conde 1982-83,
- Don Masson 1983,
- Dave Needham 1983-86,
- Alan Buckley 1986-88,
- Peter Morris 1988-92,
- David Cusack 1992,
- Graham Carr 1992-95,
- Gary Johnson 1995-96,
- Steve Berry 1996-98,
- Peter Morris 1998-

MANAGER OF THE MONTH AWARDS. Colin Clarke - September and March, 1980-81. Dave Needham - December, 1984-85. Alan Buckley - October* and March, 1987-88 (* joint with Colin Murphy of Lincoln City). Peter Morris - September, 1990-91. Graham Carr - April, 1993-94. Steve Berry - March 1997-98

MANN ARTHUR. Full back. Born Falkirk. Previous clubs: Hearts, Manchester City, Notts County, Shrewsbury Town, Mansfield Town, Boston United and Telford United. Arthur originally joined the Poppies in the summer of 1983, but had moved to Boston United by October. He became United's player/manager before a spell at Telford United then returning to Rockingham Road in 1985. Passionate, solid performer who gave his all for the club. Had a short period as caretaker manager of the Poppies with Billy Jeffrey - winning their first game in charge, a 5-1 win over Welling United just four days after the 0-8 thrashing by Sutton United during the 1986-87 season. Arthur was sadly missed when he left the club to become Alan Buckley's assistant manager at Grimsby Town at the end of the 1987-88 season. Later followed Buckley to WBA.

Alliance Premier League, debut v Scarborough (h) 20:08:83

Appearances: 113   League 85+2   **Goals:** 0
Cups   26

MARCH JAMIE. Fullback. Born Leicester. Previous club: Friar Lane Old Boys. Signed during the 1995-96 close season by Gary Johnson. Originally a schoolboy trialist with Leicester City, Jamie played for local Leicester sides before a trial spell at Port Vale as a seventeen year old. Broke into the Poppies first team during his first season at the club improving each game. Such was his improvement he was placed on standby for the prestigious Middlesex Wanderers Summer 1996 tour to Vietnam, unfortunately everybody was fit and Jamie did not go. Had the dinstinction of playing the last five minutes of a Northants Senior Cup 2nd Round match, in goal due to an injury to Kevin Shoemake - the Poppies won 2-1, thanks to last gasp goal by Carl Alford. Continued in the first team during the 1996-97 season but was freed by the club at the end of the campaign. Joined Stevenage Borough after leaving the Poppies.

Debut (County Cup) v Rushden & Diamonds (a) 27:07:95
GM Vauxhall Conference, debut v Altrincham (a) 19:08:95

Appearances: 74   League 40+18   **Goals:** 0
Cups   9+7

MARSHALL ROB. Full back. Previous clubs: Watford and Harrow Borough. Signed for the Poppies during the 1996-97 close season by Gary Johnson. This 6'1" right back played most of his games at Watford in the reserves and a loan spell at Harrow Borough before his move to Rockingham Road. After just one season at the club he joined Stevenage Borough in a swap deal during the 1997-98 close season that brought Robbie Mutchell to Rockingham Road.

GM Vauxhall Conference, debut v Macclesfield Town (a) 17:08:96

Appearances: 46   League 36+2   **Goals:** 0
Cups   8

MARTIN DEAN. Winger. Born London. Previous clubs: West Ham United, Fisher Athletic and Colchester United. 'Deano' originally joined the club on loan during 1992 but rejoined the U's. Signed for the Poppies in July 1993 on a permanent basis but after a promising start, he never recaptured his earlier brilliance. An enigma to many, Dean left the club under a shroud of mystery midway through the 1994-95 season and joined Welling United, then later Dagenham & Redbridge, where he played for both clubs against the Poppies. Later played for Brentford.

GM Vauxhall Conference, debut v Welling United (h) 05:12:92

Appearances: 53   League 32+11   **Goals:** 7   League 6
Cups   9+1   Cups   1

MARTIN DENNIS. Winger. Born Edinburgh. Previous clubs: West Bromwich Albion, Carlisle United, Newcastle United, Mansfield Town and Fremad Amager (Denmark). Began his career with the Poppies making 84 Southern League appearances, scoring 16 goals before a move to West Bromwich Albion. Rejoined Kettering from Mansfield Town - staying just one season. Dennis scored his first Alliance goal for the club in the 4-0 home demolition of Yeovil Town during the 1980-81 season.

Southern League Division One, debut v Bath City (a) 04:09:65
Alliance Premier League, debut v Worcester City (a) 16:08:80

Appearances: 45   League 29 + 3   **Goals:** 3   League 3
Cups   13

MARTIN MICK. Diminutive goalkeeper. Previous clubs: Nuneaton Borough and VS Rugby. Mick played during the 1993-94 season against Welling United (another goalkeeping crisis), the

Poppies drew 2-2, both of Welling's goals were credited as own goals by Kettering players.

GM Vauxhall Conference, debut v Welling United (h) 18:12:93

Appearances: 1   League 1

Cups   0

MASON PHIL. Defender. Born Consett. Previous club: Newcastle United where he played in the youth and reserve sides before being released. Made just one appearance for the Poppies in the 1993-94 Maunsell Cup 2-0 success against Northampton Town. Phil was injured in training, never to be seen in Kettering's colours again. Joined Spennymore United after leaving the Poppies and later played for Worcester City.

Debut (Maunsell Cup) v Northampton Town (h) 07:08:93

Appearances: 1   League 0   **Goals:** 0

Cups   1

MASSEY RICHARD. Defender. Born Wolverhampton. Signed by Peter Morris during the 1988-89 close season from Exeter City. Richard made his debut in the opening day of the season but, after failing to gain a regular first team place, joined Stourbridge.

Debut (Maunsell Cup) v Peterborough United (h) 13:08:88

GM Vauxhall Conference, debut v Northwich Victoria (h) 20:08:88

Appearances: 11   League 6+1   **Goals:** 0

Cups   3+1

MASSON DON. Player/manager. Joined the club in March 1983 after the sacking of Jim Conde. A former Scottish international midfielder who had played for Middlesbrough, Notts County (twice), Queens Park Rangers, Derby County and Bulova (Hong Kong). Don's first signing was former Arsenal player Eddie Kelly and first game in charge of the club was the 3-2 away win at Underhill, Barnet in April 1983. Masson had to fight a relegation battle right up to the wire. The Poppies lost their last two games of the 1982-83 season but results went the Poppies way, finally securing Alliance survival by 4 points. After a series of poor performances the following season and another dog fight to stay in the top flight of non-league football, after allegedly poor training, Masson was sacked and replaced by Dave Needham and Peter Denyer in a temporary role. Needham eventually becoming the manager and Denyer his assistant. Don scored his only goal for the Poppies in the 2-1 home win against Boston United.

Alliance Premier League, debut v Scarborough (h) 20:08:83

Appearances: 6   League 5+1   *Goals:* 1   League 1
                          Cups   0

MANAGERIAL RECORD
April to October 1983

	P	W	D	L	F	A
League	19	7	1	11	27	37
Cups	3	1	1	1	7	6
TOTAL	**22**	**8**	**2**	**12**	**34**	**43**

Don Masson

MAUNSELL CUP. The winners of the Northamptonshire Hillier Senior Cup compete against either Northampton Town or Peterborough United for the Maunsell Cup. Since 1979 Kettering have won this competition on five occasions having reached the final nine times.

Season	Venue	Opponents	F-A
1984-85	H	Peterborough Utd	1-1
			(4-2 on penalties)
1987-88	H	Northampton Town	1-0
1988-89	H	Peterborough Utd	3-0
1992-93	H	Peterborough Utd	1-0
1993-94	H	Northampton Town	2-0

The highest attendance is 1,818 against Northampton Town in season 1993-94 and the lowest is 617 against Peterborough in 1986-87, the Posh winning 1-0.

The leading goalscorer is Robbie Cooke with 2 goals. Nine other players have each scored once.

MAYES BOBBY. Forward. Previous clubs: West Ham United, FC Boon (Belgium) and Bury Town. A Peter Morris close season signing during the summer of 1989 from non-league Bury Town. Bobby made his only Conference start in the 0-2 home defeat by Kidderminster Harriers and a substitute appearance five days later during the 0-3 defeat at Welling United. Went on later to play for Wivenhoe Town and Redbridge Forest, banging in a superb volley for Forest in their 4-0 demolition of the Poppies in season 1991-92. Later played in the Chelmsford City side that knocked the Poppies out of the 1996-97 FA Trophy.

GM Vauxhall Conference, debut v Kidderminster Harriers (h) 28:08:89

Appearances: 2   League 1+1   **Goals:** 0
                       Cups   0

MAY LEROY. Forward. Born Wolverhampton. Previous clubs: Kidderminster Harriers, Stafford Rangers, Hereford United, Walsall and Altrincham. A striker signed from Kidderminster Harriers for £10,000 (would have risen to £15,000 after 25/50 first team appearances, this was not to be) by Gary Johnson during the 1996-97 season. His early Poppies career faltered due to injury but when he was fit he opened his goal scoring account with a brace against

Atherstone United in the FA Cup 2nd Qualifying Round replay and later the winner against rivals Rushden & Diamonds in the Northants Hillier Senior Cup 2nd Round. After a poor run in the team, manager Steve Berry terminated Leroy's contract during the Christmas period. Later joined Enfield for £7,000.

GM Vauxhall Conference, debut v Southport (h) 21:09:96

Appearances: 17   League 10+1   **Goals:** 6   League 2
                     Cups   6   Cups   4

McGOLDRICK EDDIE. Full back. Born London. Previous club: Peterborough United. Eddie played for the Poppies as a 17year old full-back and was class even in his early days. Made his debut during the 1981-82 season at Moss Lane, Altrincham - the Poppies losing 1-2. After three seasons, a prized asset, he was allowed to join rivals Nuneaton Borough, whose manager was Graham Carr - he couldn't believe his luck when he captured Eddie, so he told me. Later played for Crystal Palace, Arsenal, Manchester City and Stockport County.

Alliance Premier League, debut v Altrincham (a) 30:01:82

Appearances: 110   League 88 + 2   **Goals:** 9   League 4
                       Cups   19 + 1   Cups   5

MERGER.   A possible merger with Northampton Town was discussed in 1985 as both the Poppies and Cobblers were finding times hard. The new team was to be called 'Northants County' with home matches played at Rockingham Road. Both clubs and sets of supporters objected to this amalgamation and the idea was soon dropped. The second possible merger was muted in the local press in 1997 by the Kettering Town Chairman. This time the merger was going to be with arch rivals Corby Town, based at Rockingham Triangle, with alleged Corby Council support to develop the stadium. This like the last time a merger was mentioned, fuelled the fans into a frenzy of activity, in Kettering's case 95% of the fans opposed a move out of town, but did realise the need to find a new home within the Borough. The Corby Town option was finally ended after much opposition from the Kettering Town (Poppies) Supporter's Trust. There was even the possibility of an alleged Trust financial package buy out option if the Corby proposal went ahead.

Currently the club is still housed at Rockingham Road with all the indications that a future site within the Borough has been found, most likely at the Old Cohen's Yard breakers facility, just off the A14.

McGOWAN ANDY. Midfield. Born Corby. Previous clubs: Kidderminster Harriers, Northampton Town, Corby Town, Rushden Town and Stamford. Played in the 1980 FA Vase final on the victorious Stamford side. Andy scored a last minute equaliser at Altrincham on his debut in August 1985. His final goal for the club also came against Altrincham during October in the Poppies 2-2 draw at Rockingham Road.

Gola League, debut v Altrincham (a) 24:08:85

Appearances: 17   League 15   **Goals:** 3   League 3
Cups   2

McINTOSH MALCOLM. Full Back. Previous club: Oxford United. Joined the Poppies from Oxford during the summer of 1981 and after one season left the club during the 1982-83 close season.

Alliance Premier League, debut v Maidstone United (h) 15:08:82

Appearances: 49   League 40 **Goals:** 0
Cups   9

McKERNON CRAIG. Full back. Previous clubs: Mansfield Town, Arsenal, Tamworth and Shepshed Albion. Serious injury forced Craig out of full time football with Arsenal. Signed by Graham Carr during the 1992-93 season from Shepshed. At the height of his career he was involved in a £250,000 move from Mansfield Town to Arsenal.

GM Vauxhall Conference, debut v Bromsgrove Rovers (a) 23:01:93

Appearances: 10   League 7+1   **Goals:** 0
Cups   2

McILROY STEVE. Forward. A product of the Kettering Town youth team, who joined Dunstable on a permanent basis in 1980 after a loan spell. Scored two of his three Kettering goals in the 4-1 away win at Worcester City in March 1980.

Alliance Premier League, debut v Altrincham (a) 03:03:80

Appearances: 10   League 8 **Goals:** 3   League 3
Cups   2

McLLWAIN ALAN. Full-back. Born Corby. Previous clubs: Corby Town and Stamford. Played for the Lincolnshire side in the 1984 FA Vase Final. Rejoined Corby Town during the 1986-87

90

close season. Known for a controversial sending off at Chelmsford City in the FA Cup 4th Qualifying Round in October 1985, the Poppies going down 0-1.

Gola League, debut v Altrincham (a) 24:08:85

Appearances: 30   League 20+1   *Goals:* 0
                        Cups   9

McMAHON SAM*. Midfield. Born Newark. Previous club: Leicester City. Signed on loan from Leicester by Steve Berry during January 1997. After five impressive games Sam was recalled by Leicester on the eve of a Conference match.

GM Vauxhall Conference debut v Northwich Victoria (a) 11:01:97

Appearances: 5   League 4   *Goals:* 0
                       Cups   1

McPARLAND IAN. Striker. Born Edinburgh. Previous clubs. Notts County, Hull City, Walsall and Dunfermline. Signed during the 1995-96 season by Gary Johnson making his debut as a second half substitute in the 2-4 away defeat at Runcorn. Later the same season he signed for Dagenham & Redbridge playing one game.

GM Vauxhall Conference, debut v Runcorn (a) 28:10:95

Appearances: 3   League 0+3   *Goals:* 0
                       Cups   0

MIDDLETON JOEY. Defender. A product of the Kettering Town youth team, given first team opportunities by Colin Clarke. Joey's only goal and claim to fame was scored against Maidstone United in the FA Cup 1st Round second replay, during the 1980-81 season. Made his only Alliance appearance against Altrincham at Rockingham Road, the Poppies drew 1-1.

Debut (FA Cup) v Maidstone United (a) 26:11:80
Alliance Premier League, debut v Altrincham (h) 29:11:80

Appearances: 4   League 1   *Goals:* 1   League 0
                       Cups   2+1   Cups   1

MILES PAUL. Defender. Born Haverhill. Signed as an apprentice during the 1995-96 season from the youth team. Made his debut for the club in the Northants Senior Cup, going on to make a few appearances in the Vauxhall Conference towards the end of the 95-96 season, likewise the 96-97 season. Paul's career as a bit part player continued under Steve Berry as the youngster made 16 appearances during the difficult 1997-98 season.

Debut (County Cup) v Rothwell Town (a) 27:02:96
GM Vauxhall Conference, debut v Halifax Town (a) 08:04:96
Appearances: 24   League 1+14   **Goals:** 0
Cups   6+3

MILKINS JOHN*. Goalkeeper. Previous clubs: Portsmouth and Oxford United. Joined the Poppies from Oxford on loan, during the 1979-80 season. Made his debut in January at Holker Street, Barrow - the Poppies won 2-1. John went through February without conceding a goal, he added one more game in March before Worcester City put four past him ending his five game clean sheet run. Returned to Oxford United, just before the end of the season.
Alliance Premier League, debut v Barrow (a) 19:01:80
Appearances: 17   League 14
Cups   3

MILLER CHRIS. Goalkeeper. Signed during yet another goalkeeping crisis during the 1995-96 season, making his debut in the first half against Bath City in place of the injured Alan Judge, as second choice goalkeeper Kevin Shoemake was also on the injury list. Chris' first act was to pick the ball out of the net as the Romans went on to win 3-1.
GM Vauxhall Conference, debut v Bath City (a) 09:12:95
Appearances: 1   League 0+1
Cups   0

MOODIE MICK. Left back. A product of the Kettering Town youth team making just two appearances during the 1979-80 season.
Alliance Premier League, debut v Altrincham (a) 03:03:80
Appearances: 2   League 2   **Goals:** 0
Cups   0

MOORE DAVID. Midfield. Born Birmingham. Previous clubs. Aston Villa and Worcester City. A Steve Berry signing in December 1997 from Worcester City, prior to his time at St George's Lane he played in Finland.
GM Vauxhall Conference, debut v Halifax Town (a) 20:12:97
Appearances: 18   League 14   **Goals:** 0
Cups   2

MORAN RITCHIE. Forward. Previous clubs: Fareham Town, Gosport Borough, Fujita (Japan) and Birmingham City. Forward signed by Peter Morris from Birmingham during the 1990-91 season. If you did not go to the away fixtures then you would not have seen Ritchie in a Poppies shirt. His second appearance was in the 2-3 defeat by Emley in the FA Trophy 3rd Round.

GM Vauxhall Conference, debut v Cheltenham Town (a) 16:02:91

Appearances: 2   League 1   **Goals:** 0
Cups   1

MORRIS PETER. Born Mansfield. In terms of team consistency, Peter Morris is the most successful manager since Ron Atkinson's reign at the club in the 1970's. An experienced player with Mansfield Town, Ipswich Town and Norwich City. A former manager of Mansfield Town, Peterborough United, Crewe Alexandra, Southend United and Nuneaton Borough. Joined the Poppies after a spell as assistant manager to Bryan Hamilton at Leicester City. Peter was installed as the new Kettering Town manager in 1988 after Alan Buckley left the club to join Grimsby Town. Peter's first major decision was to sell Poppies favourite Frankie Murphy for £10,000 to Barnet and with only 4 contracted players left in his squad, he had major rebuilding plans ahead. Never out of the top five position, he finished runner-up to Maidstone United - his first season in charge. Good FA Cup runs, healthy attendances (league average for his four seasons in charge - 2,291), good transfer market trade, the Poppies and town were a major force during his four season tenure. Resigned during Brian Talbot and Mark English's involvement with the club, during the 1992-93 close season. Went on to manage Boston United, Northampton Town (caretaker) and King's Lynn. After six seasons away from Rockingham Road, Peter Morris returned as manager in May 1998, to continue his love affair with the Poppies after Steve Berry's departure.

Honours won: Northants Senior Cup. 1989-90, 1991-92.
Maunsell Cup, 1988-89.

MANAGERIAL RECORD
July 1988 to May 1992

	P	W	D	L	F	A
League	166	84	43	39	261	187
Cups	49	26	8	15	79	59
TOTAL	**215**	**110**	**51**	**54**	**340**	**246**

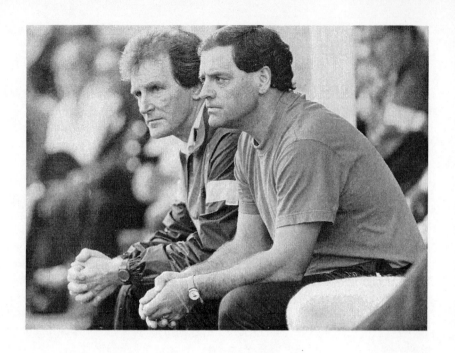

Peter Morris - the most successful Poppies manager since 1979, sat alongside physio Ritchie Norman.

MORTIMER DENNIS. Midfield. Previous clubs. Brighton Hove Albion, Aston Villa and Birmingham City. While at Villa he captained the 1981 European Cup winning side that beat Bayern Munich 1-0. Dennis joined Kettering after being released by Birmingham in July 1987. After playing just over half the 1987-88 season Dennis left the Poppies to take over as the player/manager of Redditch United.

Debut (Maunsell Cup) v Northampton Town (h) 08:08:87
GM Vauxhall Conference, debut v Enfield (h) 22:08:87
Appearances: 29   League 22 **Goals:** 0
Cups 7

MOSS ERNIE. Centre forward. Born Chesterfield. Previous clubs: Chesterfield, Peterborough United, Port Vale, Lincoln City, Doncaster Rovers, Stockport County, Scarborough and Shepshed Charterhouse. Another one of Peter Morris's first signings when he took over as manager during the summer of 1988. Ernie joined the club from Scarborough and became a folk hero to the people of Kettering, with his professional attitude and application in front of goal along with partner Robbie Cooke he featured in some classic matches during the good times in the more recent years of Kettering Town FC. His goal and as it turned out winner, on his return against Boston on 1st January 1991 at York Street sent the 1000+ travelling fans into a thriving mass of red. A great ambassador of the game and sadly missed, joined Peter Morris at Boston United in season 1992-93. Later managed Gainsborough and Leek Town.

GM Vauxhall Conference, debut v Northwich Victoria (h) 20:08:88

Appearances: 99   League 70+7   **Goals:** 28 League 23
Cups   11+2   Cups   5

Ernie Moss - a former crowd favourite.

MUCKLEBERG TERRY. Full-back. Previous clubs: Oxford United, Banbury United, Oxford City, Brackley Town and Buckingham Town. Signed during the 1993-94 close season from Buckingham Town by Graham Carr. Made a promising debut against Welling United in the BLT but could not claim a regular first team birth. Made his last appearance for the club in the 0-3 defeat at Kidderminster Harriers in the FA Cup 1st Round. Later joined Marlow.

Debut (League Cup) v Welling United (h) 07:09:93
GM Vauxhall Conference, debut v Stalybridge Celtic (a) 06:11:93
Appearances: 4   League 0+1   **Goals:** 0
                        Cups   3

MUIR MAURICE. Forward. Joined the club from Northampton Town during the 1984-85 pre-season. Maurice's only goal for the club was scored against Dartford in the Gola League, as it turned out the only goal of the game. Maurice will always remember the goal, not only scoring for Kettering but getting knocked out and carried off. Well he might remember parts of it.

Gola League, debut v Dagenham (a) 22:08:84
Appearances: 10   League 3+5   **Goals:** 1   League 1
                        Cups   1+1

MURPHY FRANK. Striker. Born Glasgow. Previous clubs: Desborough Town, Corby Town, Nuneaton Borough and Barnet. Joined the Poppies originally from Desborough Town for a £2,000 installment paid fee. A stylish goal scorer who currently leads the Poppies hot shot chart since 1979 with 82 goals. Frankie scored two hat-tricks in his Poppies career and holds the distinction of being the only Kettering player since 1979 to have scored three in a game and ended up on the losing side, a 3-4 home defeat by Bangor City. Left Kettering for Nuneaton, returning  under the managership of Alan Buckley, only for Peter Morris to sell him to Barnet for £10,000. He reappeared for a final time under Graham Carr's 1992-93 great escape campaign. Murphy will always be remembered by the Poppies faithful - a true hero and class player.

Alliance Premier League, debut v Maidstone United (h) 15:08:81
Appearances: 185   League 144+6   **Goals:** 82   League 72
                         Cups   33+2   Cups   10

MURPHY MATT*. Striker. Born Northampton. Previous clubs: Corby Town and Oxford United. Signed by Graham Carr on loan from Oxford United during the 1992-93 season. During his short stay with the club he showed little of his undoubted ability, finally going back to Oxford at the end of his spell.

GM Vauxhall Conference, debut v Yeovil Town (a) 29:01:94

Appearances: 6   League 3+2   **Goals:** 0
Cups   1

MUSTAFA TARKAN. Winger. Born London. Previous club: Leyton FC. Tarkan was a Gary Johnson signing during the 1995-96 close season. An exciting winger who never fullfilled his true potential. Set the crowds alight with excellent performances against Luton, WBA and Arsenal during pre-season, but a stress fracture to his ankle limited his performances during the GMVC campaign. Made a good start to the 1996-97 season but tailed off again due to injury, another disappointing campaign led to Tarkan being released. Later played for Barnet.

Debut (County Cup) v Rushden & Diamonds (a) 27:07:95
GM Vauxhall Conference, debut v Altrincham (a) 19:08:95

Appearances: 74   League 50+10   **Goals:** 10 League 8
Cups   13+1   Cups   2

MUTCHELL ROBBIE. Left back: Born Solihull. Previous clubs: Stevenage Borough, Telford United and Barnet. Steve Berry's first close season signing/exchange deal with Rob Marshall, from previous club Stevenage Borough, where he played alongside Robbie in Borough's Vauxhall Conference championship side during the 1995-96 season. An ever present in the Poppies team, he only missed one game all season, due to suspension, playing in 53 of the 54. He was voted the players 'Player of the Season'. Robbie scored his first goal for the club in the 1-0 home win over Dorchester in the First Round of the FA Trophy.

Debut (Maunsell Cup) v Northampton Town (h) 29:07:97
GM Vauxhall Conference, debut v Slough Town (h) 16:08:97

Appearances: 53   League 41   **Goals:** 3 League 2
Cups   12   Cups   1

N

NAYLOR STUART*. Goalkeeper signed on loan from Lincoln City by Jim Conde during January 1983. Made just two appearances during the 1982-83 season.

Alliance Premier League, debut v Stafford Rangers (h) 05:02:83

Appearances: 2   League 2
                       Cups   0

Dave Needham

NEEDHAM DAVE. Player/manager, Central defender. Born Leicester. Previous clubs: Notts County, QPR, Nottingham Forest and Toronto Blizzard (Canada), also an England 'B' International. Nott'm Forest paid £150,000 to QPR for his services. Joined the

Poppies in pre-season 1983 and appointed manager of Kettering in October 1983 in succession to Don Masson, the man who had brought him to Kettering. Dave had to fight an instant relegation battle which was only resloved in the penultimate game of the season, even then the Poppies lost 0-2 at Yeovil Town but survived (as only two teams were to be relegated that season). Needham's career saw more downs than ups, a 0-7 home thrashing by Swindon in the FA Cup 1st Round during his first season in charge and two seasons later the clubs worst performance in the Conference an 0-8 away thrashing at Sutton United that finally killed Needham off along with friend and coach Jon Nixon. Scored his only Alliance goal in the 2-2 draw at Rockingham Road against Dagenham. His other goal was scored in the FA Cup 4th Qualifying Round against Sutton Coldfield Town. The Poppies won 3-2. Needham was the last player/manager of Kettering until season 1996-97 when Steve Berry entered the fray.

Alliance Premier League, debut v Scarborough (h) 20:08:83

Appearances: 22   League 16+1   **Goals:** 2   League 1
                          Cups   5   Cups   1
Honours won: Northants Senior Cup, 1983-84, 1984-85.
                   Maunsell Cup, 1984-85.

MANAGERIAL RECORD
October 1983 to October 1986

	P	W	D	L	F	A
League	130	41	38	51	180	193
Cups	37	18	9	10	57	50
TOTAL	167	59	47	61	237	243

NEVILLE CHRIS. Goalkeeper. The former Ipswich Town player was signed by Peter Morris. Chris saved a penalty on his debut against Boston United in the 1-1 draw at Rockingham Road during the 1990-91 season. But was never given a chance to claim a regular first team spot, with Kevin Blackwell as Morris's number one.

GM Vauxhall Conference, debut v Boston United (h) 26:12:90

Appearances: 7   League 3
                        Cups   4

NICKNAME - 'The Poppies'. The Poppies nickname goes back, allegedly, to a reporter called the Friar, who coined a phrase before the First World War that included the colour of Kettering's shirts being 'Poppy red'. There have been more romantic stories, that the club used to play on a Poppy Field and the roads into Kettering were always lined with Poppy fields. But the Friars name struck a chord before those theories and is the one used today.

NICOL PAUL. Central defender. Born Scunthorpe. A Peter Morris signing during the 1990-91 close season from Scunthorpe United. Formed a good partnership with Trevor Slack and was rewarded not only as club captain but also recognition with three international caps with the England semi-professional side. Paul scored two of his three Conference goals during the 1991-92 season in consecutive games, the 3-1 home win against Merthyr Tydfil and the 1-1 draw at Boston United on Boxing Day. Left Kettering and later joined Boston United during the troubled 1992-93 season.

Debut (Maunsell Cup) v Peterborough United (h) 14:08:90
GM Vauxhall Conference, debut v Bath City (a) 18:08:90

Appearances: 139   League 107   **Goals:** 3   League *3*
                       Cups   32

NIGHTINGALE MARK. Full back. Born Salisbury. Previous clubs: Bournemouth (twice), Crystal Palace, Norwich City, Bulova (Hong Kong) and Peterborough United. Mark was one of Peter Morris's first signings during the 1988-89 close season, joining from Peterborough United. Paul's only goal for the club came against Stafford Rangers (the game ended 1-2 to Rangers) on the final weekend of the 1988-89 campaign - a season where he played in every game, the only squad player to do so.

Debut (Maunsell Cup) v Peterborough United (h) 13:08:88
GM Vauxhall Conference, debut v Northwich Victoria (h) 20:08:88

Appearances: 96   League 74+2   **Goals:** 1   League 1
                      Cups   20

NORMAN GRAIG. Full back. Born Perivale. A former Chelsea trainee and professional, spent 4 years at Stamford Bridge before joining the Poppies during the 1995-96 season. Scored one goal in his first season at Southport finishing off a good move at the near post. Craig went from strength to strength earning himself the Executive Player of the Season for 1995-96. During the 1996-7 season he continued to impress defensively as well as a goalscoring midfielder - delighting the fans with a home brace against Altrincham in the 3-1 Rockingham Road victory. He ended the season as the club's top scorer with 12 goals and the prestigious Supporters Player of the Season for 1996-97 and a consecutive Executive Player of the Season, during another difficult campaign. Craig led by example again during a relegation season battle during the 1997-98 campaign with a series of performances that impressed Leicester City's watching scouts.

GM Vauxhall Conference, debut v Morecambe (a) 14:10: 95

Appearances: 120   League 88+4   **Goals:** 23   League 18
                 Cups   26+2   Cups   5

NORTHAMPTONSHIRE HILLIER SENIOR CUP. Since 1979 the County Trophy has been won on 11 occasions.

Season	V	Opponents	F-A
1979-80	H	Irthlingborough Diamonds	3-0
1983-84	A	Long Buckby	2-1
		(after a replay, 1st game 2-2)	
1984-85	H	Irthlingborough Diamonds	2-2
		(4-2 on penalties)	
1986-87	A	Corby Town	2-1
1987-88	H	Rothwell Town	2-1
1989-90	H	Northampton Spencer	3-2
1991-92	H	Corby Town	1-0
1992-93	H	Rushden & Diamonds	2-1
1994-95	H	Rushden & Diamonds	2-2
		(4-2 on penalties, after a 2-2 draw at Nene Park).	
1996-97	H	Daventry Ford Sports	3-1
1997-98	H	Raunds Town	2-1

The leading goalscorers in the competition are Frankie Murphy with 6, Eddie McGoldrick, David Hofbauer, Mark Smith and Tim Wilkes with 4, Phil Brown and Chris Pearson on 3.

Leading appearances are Doug Keast with 9, Phil Brown, David Hofbauer, Frankie Murphy and Mark Smith with 7, and Sean Suddards with 6.

The highest Rockingham Road gate in the competition is 1,837 v Rushden & Diamonds in 1996-97 (2nd Round), the lowest 344 v Rothwell Town in the 1984-85 semi-final.

NORTH MARC. Striker. Born Ware. Previous clubs: Grimsby Town, Leicester City and Shepshed Albion. A Peter Morris signing, originally Marc joined the Poppies from Shepshed Albion during the

1991-92 season and made an immediate impact scoring two goals against Cheltenham Town, (as a substitute), he tried to claim all three goals for the obvious hat-trick but Richard Huxford, who also got a faint touch on the ball, claimed the other goal. He returned for a second spell under Graham Carr during the 1992-93 season.

GM Vauxhall Conference, debut v Cheltenham Town (h) 31:03:92

Appearances: 15 League 9+4 **Goals:** 6 League 6
Cups 2

NUGENT RICHARD. Central defender. Born Birmingham. Previous clubs: Yeovil Town, Stevenage Borough, Woking, Hitchin, Vauxhall Motors, Royston, St Albans and Barnet. A close season signing by Gary Johnson during the summer of 1996. Richard spent the latter part of the 1995-96 season at Yeovil after being released by Stevenage Borough. Chipped in with some handy goals during his first season, the first in the 4-1 home win against Halifax Town. After differing opinions, allegedly with manager Steve Berry, Nugent was allowed to join ICIS side Hendon.

GM Vauxhall Conference, debut v Macclesfield Town (a) 17:08:96

Appearances: 35 League 26 **Goals:** 4 League 3
Cups 9 Cups 1

NUTTELL MICKY. Striker. Born Boston. Previous clubs: Boston United, Carlisle United, Wycombe Wanderers, Cheltenham Town, Peterborough United, Dagenham & Redbridge, Rushden & Diamonds and Burton Albion. Re-signed by Steve Berry in August 1997 for £7,500 from Burton Albion having originally signed by Dave Cusack during the 1992-93 pre-season. After a lengthy suspension period due to his time at Boston, when Micky finally made his league debut he did so in style, scoring the winning goal against Farnborough. But barely 24 hours had past when a deal was done and he moved to Dagenham & Redbridge. Injury throughout the 1997-98 season curtailed Micky's appearances and just 2 goals, the winner and only goal against Mirrlees Blackstone in the FA Cup 1st Qualifying Round (Kettering's first win of the seaon).

Debut (Maunsell Cup) v Peterborough United (h) 08:08:92
GM Vauxhall Conference, debut v Farnborough Town (h) 08:08:92

Appearances: 23 League 13+4 **Goals:** 3 League 2
Cups 4+2 Cups 1

NYAMAH KOFI. Midfield. Born Islington. Previous clubs: Cambridge United, Stevenage Borough (loan). A Gary Johnson signing from former club Cambridge United during the 1995-96 close season. Originally Kofi was played out of position for the Poppies as a left back but when he was put in his preferred position (in midfield or on the wing) he began to shine. Kofi was sent off (unluckily) on his Conference debut against Altrincham on the opening day of the 1995-96 season. He later scored a brace of goals against Macclesfield Town to put the Poppies 2-0 ahead in March 1996 but the Silkmen fought back to draw 2-2. Made an impressive start to the 1996-97 season which saw a move to Endsleigh League Division One side Stoke City for an initial fee of £25,000 during December 1996.

Debut (County Cup) v Rushden & Diamonds (a) 27:07:95
GM Vauxhall Conference, debut v Altrincham (a) 19:08:95

Appearances: 68   League 51   **Goals:** 6   League 5
Cups   17   Cups   1

O

O'KEEFE TERRY. Forward. Scored a hat-trick against Luton Town Reserves in a friendly in February 1984 - his only goals for a first team XI. Made his first team debut for the club on the final day of 1983, away at Weymouth - the Poppies drew 1-1.

Alliance Premier League, debut v Weymouth (a) 31:12:83

Appearances: 7   League 6+1   **Goals:** 0

Cups   0

OLDEST PLAYER. Ernie Moss at 41 and 169 days is the holder of this particular record. Ernie's last game for the club was against Telford United at Rockingham Road on Saturday April 6th 1991, although he made a guest appearance for the club in Phil Brown's testimonial game at the end of the 1995-96 season.

O'RILEY DAVE. Midfield. A forward signed by Colin Clarke from Aylesbury United during the 1981-82 pre-season period. Played the first three games of the 1981-82 season but was never on a winning side for the Poppies.

Alliance Premier League, debut v Maidstone United (h) 15:08:82

Appearances: 4   League 3+1   **Goals:** 0

Cups   0

OXBROW DARREN. Central defender. Born Ipswich. Previous clubs: Ipswich Town, Maidstone United and Barnet. Originally joined the Poppies on loan from Barnet during the 1992-93 season. Darren had the misfortune of scoring an own goal for Maidstone against Kettering during the Poppies 2-1 away win in the FA Cup 2nd Round in 1990-91. Darren must hold one of the most unique records in first class football, of being sent off twice (Altrincham and Bath City) and having both decisions reversed in his favour. Rejoined the Poppies for the third time in 1995-96 after leaving through work commitments the season before. Darren was released during the 1996-97 close season.

GM Vauxhall Conference, debut v Stalybridge Celtic (h) 03:04:93

Appearances: 99   League 79+1   ***Goals:*** 9   League 7
                      Cups   18+1   Cups   2

P

PACK LENNY. Midfielder. Born Sailsbury. Previous Club Cambridge United. Brought into the side by Steve Berry making his debut in the Spalding Challenge Cup, a tie Kettering won 3-1

Debut (League Cup) v Dover Athletic (a) 07:10:97

Appearances: 1   League 0   **Goals:** 0
               Cups   1

PALGRAVE BRIAN. Striker. Born Birmingham Previous clubs: Alvechurch, Nuneaton Borough and Bromsgrove Rovers. Brian made his only appearance as a second half substitute against Bath City during the 1987-88 season, The Romans won 2-0 at Twerton Park. Brian left for the pastures of Port Vale.

GM Vauxhall Conference, debut v Bath City (a) 21:11:87

Appearances: 1   League 0+1   **Goals:** 0
               Cups   0

PALMER JEM. Central defender. Born Kettering. Previous club: Desborough Town. One of the few locally born players to make the grade with Kettering Town. Jem joined the Poppies from Desborough in the 1982 close season. A former team captain who made his debut in 1982-83. Scored his first Alliance Premier League goal in the 3-1 home win against Runcorn during the 1982-83 season. Jem later moved to Corby Town during December 1984.

Alliance Premier League, debut v Trowbridge (h) 14:08:83

Appearances: 86   League 57+12   **Goals:** 3   League 2
               Cups   15+ 2   Cups   1

PARSONS MARK. Fullback. Born Luton. Previous club: Northampton Town. Mark was signed by Graham Carr during the 1994-95 pre-season, but had to wait eight months to make his Conference debut. Hit a super goal at Bath City during the 1-3

106

defeat in the 1995-96 season, a half volley from 20-yards. Mark was unable to establish a regular first team place, he joined Cambridge City in January 1996. Later played for Hitchin.

GM Vauxhall Conference, debut v Kidderminster Harriers (a) 04:05:95

Appearances: 13   League 4+5   ***Goals:*** 1   League 1
                Cups   3+1   Cups   0

PAWLUK ANDY. A Kettering Town reserve player whose only appearance was as a substitute against Runcorn during the 1982-83 season. One he would wish to forget as the Poppies were thrashed 6-0 at Canal Street, the Poppies second worst result in the league to date.

Alliance Premier League, debut v Runcorn (a) 05:10:82

Appearances: 1   League 0+1   ***Goals:*** 0
               Cups 0

PEARSON CHRIS. Striker. Born Leicester. Previous clubs: Notts County and Hinckley Town. Steve Berry's first signing in 1997 when the former Notts County youth and reserve team player left mid-placed Hinckley Town of the Dr Marten's Midland Division to join the Poppies in January. Chris became the 30th player to score on his debut and the third against Northwich Victoria when he did so in the 20th minute at Drill Field in January. Added two more goals to his tally in the 3-1 defeat of Ford Sports in the Northants Hillier Senior Cup. Spent a part of the 1997-98 season on loan at Eastwood Town before returning to the Poppies as a revitalised striker, notching 14 goals (a brace against Gateshead) and the mantle as the clubs leading scorer. Chris won the Executive Member's Player of the Season and the Chris Gracey, Travel Club Player of the Season Awards, but despite this he left the club for rivals Stevenage borough during the 1998-99 close season, the fee £14,000 set by a tribunal.

GM Vauxhall debut v Northwich Victoria (a) 11:01:97

Appearances: 54   League 44+3   ***Goals:*** 21   League 18
               Cups   5+2   Cups   3

PENALTIES. The Poppies longest league spell without a penalty decision was from January 28th 1995 (v Farnborough Town, Ian Arnold scored - the Poppies won 4-1) to August 20th 1996 (v Welling United, Darren Harmon scored - the Poppies losing 2-3), spanning 69 Conference games. The most conceded in a season was during the 1995-96 campaign when 11 were awarded to the opposition. Of those 11 there were 4 failures (*including a saved penalty during the abandoned Hednesford Town game). Goalkeepers Alan Judge faced 7, saving one, while Kevin Shoemake faced 4* saving three.

PERKINS GLEN*. Defender. A loan signing by Colin Clarke during December 1979 from Northampton Town. Glen made his debut for the club in the derby match against Boston United in the Poppies 3-1 win.

Alliance Premier League, debut v Boston United (h) 26:12:79

Appearances: 4   League 3   **Goals:** 0
           Cups   1

PETTINGER PAUL*. Goalkeeper. Born Sheffield. Signed on loan by Graham Carr from Leeds United during the 1994-95 season, ironically the week after Kettering had put five past him at Rockingham Road, whilst playing for Halifax Town. The Poppies were unbeaten during Paul's brief stay. Returned to Leeds after his loan spell and then obscurity, well Rotherham United actually!

GM Vauxhall Conference, debut v Altrincham (h) 18:03:95

Appearances: 5   League 5
           Cups   0

PHILLIPS BRENDAN. Midfield. Previous clubs: Peterborough United, Burton Albion and Nuneaton Borough. Stylish playmaker who joined the Poppies from Nuneaton for £5,000 during the summer of 1979 and played just the one season before being sold to Boston United for £7,000 during the 1980-81 pre-season. Scored his only league goal, (the winner as it turned out), against Northwich Victoria in the Poppies 1-0 home win. Later managed Stafford Rangers and Nuneaton Borough.

Alliance Premier League, debut v Bath City (h) 22:09:79

Appearances: 36   League 29   **Goals:** 2   League 1
           Cups   7   Cups   1

PHILLIPS IAN. Full Back. Born Kilwining. Previous clubs: Ipswich Town, Mansfield Town, Peterborough United, Northampton Town, Colchester United and Aldershot. Peter Morris brought Ian to Rockingham Road from Aldershot in the 1990-91 close season, reuniting their working relationship from the Mansfield days. After a promising start to his Poppies career serious illness forced him out of the game for a period of time, and when recovered and back in the team he was never the same player. Left to join the coaching staff at Colchester United. Once took over in goal against Stafford Rangers for the injured Kevin Shoemake - the Poppies won 2-0 at Rockingham Road.

Debut (Maunsell Cup) v Peterborough United (h) 14:08:90
GM Vauxhall Conference, debut v Bath City (a) 18:08:90

Appearances: 45   League 34+1   **Goals:** 0
Cups   10

PHIPPS PETER. Striker. Born Northampton. Previous clubs: Northampton Spencer and Irthlingborough Diamonds. Signed from Irthlingborough in 1976. Known as 'The Green Flash' after sporting a pair of green boots, that and his undoubted speed on the ball, need I say more. Perhaps one of his best games was against Worcester City, the Poppies winning 4-1, with the mighty Flash scoring two. Rejoined the Diamonds during the 1982-83 pre-season after serving six campaigns with the Poppies, (three of those in the Southern League).

Southern Premier League, debut v Maidstone United (a) 28:08:76
Alliance Premier League, debut v Stafford Rangers (a) 18:08:79

Appearances: 128   League 99+1   **Goals:** 20 League 14
Cups   28   Cups   6

PICK GARY. Midfield. Born Leicester. Previous clubs: Cambridge United, Hereford United, Shrewsbury Town, Stoke City, Leicester United, Worcester City, Cheltenham Town and Newport AFC. A Steve Berry signing during the 1997-98 close season, but after a handful of appearances was released during September 1997.

Debut (Maunsell Cup) v Northampton Town (h) 29:07:97
GM Vauxhall Conference, debut v Slough Town (h) 16:08:97

Appearances: 6   League 5   **Goals:** 0
Cups   1

PLATNAUER NICKY. Midfield. Born Leicester. Previous clubs: Bedford Town, Bristol Rovers, Coventry City, Birmingham City, Reading, Cardiff City, Notts County, Port Vale, Leicester City and Scunthorpe United. Made one competitive appearance for the Poppies during the 1993-94, 2-0 Maunsell Cup victory over Northampton Town. Joined Mansfield Town from Kettering.

Debut (Maunsell Cup) v Northampton Town (h) 08:08:93

Appearances: 1   League 0 **Goals:** 0
Cups   1

PLAYERS. The most players used during a season was 53 by a combined managerial team of Dave Cusack and Graham Carr during the 1992-93 season. The least number of players was 18 used during season 1980-81, under Colin Clarke's tenure.

PLAYER OF THE YEAR. Since 1979:
- Sean Suddards 1979-80,
- Nicky Evans 1980-81,
- Paul Haverson 1981-82,
- Jem Palmer 1982-83,
- Glynn Chamberlain 1983-84,
- Dave Wharton 1984-85,
- Tim Thacker 1985-86,
- Arthur Mann 1986-87,
- Paul Reece 1987-88,
- Russell Lewis 1988-89,
- Steve Collins 1989-90,
- Trevor Slack 1990-91,
- Richard Huxford 1991-92,
- Phil Brown 1992-93,
- Stephen Holden 1993-94,
- Phil Brown 1994-95,
- Darren Harmon 1995-96,
- Craig Norman 1996-97,
- Colin Vowden 1997-98.

POOLE ANDY. Goalkeeper. Previous clubs: Barnet, Gillingham, Wolverhampton Wanderers, Mansfield Town and Northampton Town. Andy's only game for the club came in the 1988-89 FA Cup 3rd Qualifying Round against Boreham Wood. A clean sheet for Andy as the Poppies ran out 4-0 winners.

Debut (FA Cup) v Boreham Wood (h) 15:10:88

Appearances: 1   League 0
                      Cups   1

POPE NEIL. Midfield. Born Cambridge. Previous clubs: Cambridge United, Peterborough United, Corby Town and Cambridge City. A Gary Johnson signing joining the Poppies during the 1995-96 close season for £2,000 from Cambridge City. A gritty midfielder who could be inspirational at times. After a fairly settled spell in the first team Neil was released by Steve Berry and joined Sudbury Town during December 1996. Neil scored a spectacular first goal for the club, (a bullet volley), against Southport in the 1-1 draw at Rockingham Road during the 1995-96 campaign.

Debut (County Cup) v Rushden & Diamonds (a) 27:07:95
GM Vauxhall Conference, debut v Altrincham (a) 19:08:95

Appearances: 70   League 51+1   **Goals:** 12 League 10
                        Cups   18   Cups   2

POPLAR DAVE. Forward.

Joined the Poppies from Boston United during 1982-83, a Jim Conde acquisition. Dave's only goal for Kettering came in the 4-2 home win over Bath City in 1982.

Debut (League Cup) v Bangor City (h) 25:09:82
Alliance Premier League, debut v Telford United (h) 08:09:82

Appearances: 8   League 6+1   **Goals:** 1 League 1
                       Cups   1

POWNALL DAVE. Defender.

Born Norwich. Previous clubs: Norwich City and Irthlingborough Diamonds. Joined the Poppies in the close season of 1980. Both of his goals were scored in the APL, at home to AP Leamington in the 3-0 home win in 1980 and then a three year gap - a consolation goal in the 1-3 defeat at Altrincham in 1983. Dave had the distinction of falling down when taking a penalty for Irthlingborough Diamonds against the Poppies in 1988.

Alliance Premier League, debut v Worcester City (a) 16:08:80

Appearances: 94   League 71+4   **Goals:** 2 League 2
                        Cups   19

PRICE GARETH. Full-back/midfield.

Born Swindon. Previous clubs: Mansfield Town and Bury. A Peter Morris signing during the 1991-92 season from Bury. A very popular player who showed great potential before his career was plagued with illness. Gareth played over 100 games for the club, this would have been a great deal more but for two serious illnesses the second one a tumour on the brain. Thankfully he fully recovered and re-entered the first team towards the end of the 1994-95 season. Gareth will stick in my mind for the spectacular 30 yard volley he scored against Stalybridge Celtic - stunning. After being released from the Poppies he joined Boston United after a spell on loan at Gainsborough.

GM Vauxhall Conference, debut v Altrincham (a) 17:08:91

Appearances: 121   League 85+8   **Goals:** 3 League 3
                         Cups   24+4

Q

QUICKEST GOAL. The quickest goal scored against Kettering was just 3.55 seconds by Barrow's Colin Cowperthwaite on December 8th, 1979 in the 0-4 home defeat. The Barrow striker then proceeded to score three more. Phil Brown, (although there was a claim - disputed by Phil I hasten to add- that it was an own goal by a Harriers defender), scored the Poppies quickest goal after just 21.25 seconds into the Bob Lord Trophy tie at Kidderminster Harriers during the 1994-95 season - the Poppies won 5-1.

QUINN ANDREW. Utility. A policeman signed from Shirebrook by Peter Morris during the 1991-92 season. His only game for the club came in the Northants Senior Cup semi-final against Northampton Spencer, the Poppies winning 1-0 at home.

Debut (County Cup) v Northampton Spencer (h) 04:02:92

Appearances: 1   League 0   **Goals:** 0
Cups   1

QUOW TREVOR*. Midfield. Born Peterborough. Previous clubs: Peterborough United, Gillingham and Northampton Town. A Peter Morris signing whose only goal came against Barrow in the FA Trophy 2nd Round replay at Rockingham Road during the 1990-91 season - the Poppies won 2-1 in extra time. Trevor left the Poppies after his loan spell was concluded for a brief career in Hong Kong.

GM Vauxhall Conference, debut v Yeovil Town (a) 29:09:90

Appearances: 21   League 13+4   **Goals:** 1   League 0
Cups   4   Cups   1

QUY ANDY*. Goalkeeper. Born Harlow. Previous clubs: Tottenham Hotspur, Derby County and Stalybridge Celtic. Young keeper brought in on loan by Steve Berry from Harrow Borough in September 1997. Made a good debut earning himself the man of the match. His heroics were not enough to stop the Poppies fourth consecutive home league defeat. Later signed for Hereford United.

GM Vauxhall Conference, debut v Hereford United (h) 20:09:97

Appearances: 2   League 2
Cups   0

R

RADFORD MARK. Defender. A Graham Carr signing during the 1992-93 season after a spell with Colchester United. His only league appearance was the 2-4 away defeat against Witton Albion. The only highlight that day was Frankie Murphy returning to the club and scoring the two goals in the process.

GM Vauxhall Conference, debut v Witton Albion (a) 03:10:92

Appearances: 2   League 1   **Goals:** 0
Cups   0+1

RADFORD PETER. Forward. Signed during the 1985-86 season. Made all of his appearances as a substitute.

Gola League, debut v Enfield (a) 11:09:85

Appearances: 5   League 0+4   **Goals:** 0
Cups   0+1

RAYMENT PAT. Full back.   Previous clubs: Peterborough United, Cambridge United, Corby Town and Stewart & Lloyds. The former Corby Town player/manager joined the Poppies during the 1995-96 campaign from local side Stewart & Lloyds for his first taste of Vauxhall Conference football. He left the club in March 1996 and joined Raunds Town.

GM Vauxhall Conference, debut v Farnborough Town (h) 16:12:95

Appearances: 7   League 6   **Goals:** 0
Cups   1

REA SIMON*. Central defender. Born Birmingham. A Gary Johnson signing joining the club during the 1995-96 campaign on loan from Birmingham City. Adapted well in the few games he played, but opted to go back to St Andrews after his short spell.

GM Vauxhall Conference, debut v Welling United (h) 14:11:95

Appearances: 6   League 4   **Goals:** 0
Cups   2

REDDISH SHANE. Fullback. Born Bolsover. Signed by Dave Cusack during the 1992-93 season from Doncaster Rovers. Shane deputised in goal for Paul Reece against Macclesfield Town after Reece had been sent off. Did well between the sticks as the Poppies ran out 1-0 winners. Left for Doncaster after Cusack's reign at the club ended. Later played for Northwich Victoria in the GMVC.

GM Vauxhall Conference, debut v Slough Town (a) 22:08:92
Appearances: 6   League 6   **Goals:** 0
Cups   0

Paul Reece - only goalkeeper to win the 'Player of the Year' award.

REECE PAUL. Goalkeeper. Born Nottingham. Popular teenage goalkeeper who joined the Poppies during the 1987-88 close season after being released from Stoke City. Paul made his Football League debut with the Potters having served an apprenticeship. Paul marked his Conference debut in the 2-0 York Street victory at Boston United taking over the jersey from Nick Goodwin. Left with the Alan Buckley contingent to Blundell Park,

Grimsby, costing the Mariners £10,000. During Dave Cusack's short reign at the club he rejoined the Poppies for the onset of the 1992-93 season on loan from Grimsby Town. Left Kettering after just six games and rejoined the 'Mariners'. He later followed former manager Alan Buckley to West Bromwich Albion.

Debut (Maunsell Cup) v Northampton Town (h) 08:08:87
GM Vauxhall Conference, debut v Boston United (a) 09:09:87

Appearances: 54   League 43
Cups   11

REED GRAHAM. Full back. Born Doncaster. Previous clubs: Barnsley, Northampton Town, Frickley Athletic, Aylesbury United and VS Rugby. Graham joined the club midway through the 1992-93 season and was a tower of strength during a difficult period. Reedie was promoted to club captain in 1993-94, leading his side to within 3 points of the Vauxhall Conference Championship. His equalising goal at Altrincham in the penultimate game of that season with the Poppies down to 10 men, the pure emotion and true grit etched into his face showed the determination of the man. Affectionally known to the fans as 'Rambo', injuries hampered the Yorkshireman the following season and he was released at the end of 1994-95 later joining Rushden & Diamonds for a short spell. In 1995-96 Graham once again teamed up with former Kettering Town and Northampton Town boss Graham Carr at Dagenham & Redbridge for his third spell under the Geordie.

GM Vauxhall Conference, debut v Merthyr Tydfil (h) 17:10:92

Appearances: 84   League 63+2   ***Goals:*** 3   League 2
Cups   17+2   Cups   1

REPLAYS. Ten replays have been needed in the FA Cup, the record shows the Poppies winning 4, losing 4 and drawing two. Two ties, Maidstone United and Bromsgrove Rovers have needed second replays - the Poppies losing both. Eleven replays have been needed in the FA Trophy, the Poppies coming out 6-4 ahead with one draw. Only one tie against Barking needed a second replay, the Poppies winning 2-0 on that occasion. In the League Cup three matches have gone to a replay, the Poppies winning all three encounters.

RETALLICK GRAHAM. Central defender. Born Cambridge. Previous clubs: Histon, Boston United and Peterborough United. A Graham Carr stop gap signing from Peterborough United, who made just two Conference appearances. Later went on to play for Corby Town.

GM Vauxhall Conference, debut v Altrincham (a) 09:02:93

Appearances: 2   League 2   **Goals:** 0
Cups   0

RICHARDSON   PAUL.

Central defender. Born Hucknall. Previous clubs: Nottingham Forest, Eastwood Town, Nuneaton Borough and Derby County. Paul was affectionately known by the fans as 'Tigger'. He joined the club in the 1986 close season after injury forced him out of League Football. A tough tackling 100% er who graced the Rockingham Road turf for four outstanding seasons. He scored his first goal for the club against Frickley Athletic in the 2-2 away draw during his first season with the Poppies. Paul left Kettering for Barnet during the 1990-91 season, later playing for Dagenham & Redbridge and Rushden & Diamonds - where he saw out his playing career.

GM Vauxhall Conference, debut v Weymouth (a) 16:08:86

Appearances: 162   League 117+9   **Goals:** 15   League 11
Cups   34+2   Cups   4

RICKETTS   ALAN. Forward. Previous clubs: Hitchin, Wellingborough Town and Nuneaton Borough. An Alan Buckley signing he joined the Poppies from Wellingborough in December 1987. Alan's only league start was against Fisher Athletic in the 1-1 away draw in January 1988. All his other league appearances were as a substitute. He scored his only goal for the club again as a substitute in the 1988 Northants Senior Cup Final success against Rothwell Town, the Poppies won 2-1.

GM Vauxhall Conference, debut v Wycombe Wanderers (h) 26:12:87

Appearances: 15   League 1+12   **Goals:** 1   League 0
Cups   1+1   Cups   1

RIDGWAY IAN. Winger/midfield. Born Nottingham. Previous club, Notts County. Originally a trainee at Meadow Lane where he spent three years before being released after County's relegation. Scored his first Conference goal as sustitute for player manager Steve Berry, in the 3-1 home victory over relegation bound Stalybridge Celtic. The other came in the FA Cup 2nd Qualifying Round replay against Cambridge City.

Debut (Maunsell Cup) v Northampton Town (h) 29:07:97
GM Vauxhall Conference, debut v Slough Town (h) 16:08:97

Appearances: 44   League 25+7   **Goals:** 2   League 1
         Cups   8+4   Cups   1

RILEY DAVID*.   Striker. Born Northampton. Previous clubs: Keyworth United, Nottingham Forest, Port Vale, Darlington and Peterborough United. David made quite an impact when he joined the club on loan from Peterborough United during the 1992-93 season. Scored the only goal of the game on his debut against former club Peterborough United as the Poppies lifted the Maunsell Cup in 1992. He left the Poppies to play abroad and it was hoped he would rejoin the club on a permanent basis the following season. It was quite a shock when 'Mavis' turned out for Boston United the previous season.

Debut (Maunsell Cup) v Peterborough United (h) 08:08:92
GM Vauxhall Conference, debut v Slough Town (a) 22:08:92

Appearances: 33   League 23+2   **Goals:** 11   League 9
         Cups   6   Cups   2

RITCHIE DAVID*. Striker. Signed by Peter Morris on loan from Stockport County, also played on loan for Northwich Victoria. David's only and debut goal for the club was scored away at Moss Lane against Altrincham in the Poppies 2-3 defeat during 1990-91.

GM Vauxhall Conference, debut v Altrincham (a) 26:01:91

Appearances: 1 League 1   **Goals:** 1   League 1
         Cups   0

ROBERTS DAVE. Defender. A Welsh international who had Football League experience with Cardiff City. Dave's only goal for the club was against Altrincham in the 5-4 thriller at Rockingham Road during the 1981-82 season.

Alliance Premier League, debut v Enfield (a) 12:09:81

Appearances: 3   League 2   **Goals:** 1   League 1
         Cups   1

118

ROBERTS STEVE. Defender. Signed by Jim Conde from the Poppies youth team. Made his Alliance Premier League debut (Conde's first game in charge) in the 2-3 defeat at Bath City during the 1981-82 season.

Alliance Premier League, debut v Dartford (h) 20:02:82

Appearances: 9   League 9   ***Goals:*** 0
                 Cups   0

ROCKINGHAM ROAD. Since the formation of the Alliance Premier League in 1979, there has been little visual difference to the home of Kettering Town since the Southern League days and development of the main stand. The major difference recently has been the Britannia Road side, once again being fully covered after a period of time with two half sections and a gap in the middle. More significantly was the taking down of the 'Tin Hat' covered end on Rockingham Road. This was due to the Football League 'A' grading system. This area, once the home of the Rockingham Road choir, is now normally designated for away fans. It has been re-terraced, yet remains uncovered. In between the Social Club and main stand, a 'Sponsors Lounge' has been built, while constant maintenance of the ground has continued on a regular basis to maintain the required standards. During the 1997-98 season the club celebrated 100 years at Rockingham Road having moved to the current site from North Park in 1897. After much debate and consternation during the troubled 1997-98 season Kettering Town FC look like they will be moving from their spiritual home to a brand new all purpose stadium on the boundary, south of the town, by the Millennium.

RODERICK MARTIN. Winger. Born Portsmouth. Previous clubs: Portsmouth, Wycombe Wanderers, Farnborough Town, Harrogate Town and Shepshed Albion. Signed by Graham Carr during the 1992-93 season from Shepshed Albion. After a promising start, Martin's form went right off, this was later diagnosed to be due to a serious illness that at one point was almost life threatening. 'Rodders' also represented the British Students in the World Games. Later played for Barwell in the Interlink Express League.

GM Vauxhall Conference, debut v Bromsgrove Rovers (a) 23:01:93

Appearances: 38   League 31+2   ***Goals:*** 3   League 3
                 Cups   4+1

ROWE ZEKE*. Forward. Born Stoke Newington. Previous clubs: Peterborough United, Barnet, Brighton Hove Albion and Chelsea. Striker brought on loan from Peterborough by Steve Berry in December 1997. Returned to Peterborough after just two appearances to have a knee operation. Later played for Doncaster Rovers.

GM Vauxhall Conference, debut v Farnborough Town (a) 07:09:97
Appearances: 2   League 2   **Goals:** 0

RUSHDEN & DIAMONDS - CONNECTIONS. Fifteen ex-Poppies players helped elevate our neighbours to the pinnacle of non-league football; Steve Cherry was the first ex-Poppy to join the most expensive assembled non-league side in history during their inaugural GM Vauxhall Conference season when he signed for Brian Talbot's side 48 hours after playing for Kettering against Rushden to become the 16th ex-Kettering player to join the Nene Park ranks. The full list of 18 is Carl Alford, Nick Ashby, Glenn Beech, Graham Benstead, Gary Butterworth, Steve Cherry, Glyn Creaser, Kevin Fox, Steve Holden, Ollie Kearns, Doug Keast, Micky Nuttell, Graham Reed, Paul Richardson, Kevin Shoemake, Mark Sutton, Steve Stott, Mark Turner. The signings of Mark Tucker in July and Micky Nuttall (returning) in August 1997, saw Diamonds' players signing for the Poppies - although Shoemake did return to Rockingham Road after a short spell at Nene Park.

The management team of Roger Ashby and Billy Jeffrey, both former players who feature in this book, guided them to the GMVC. Roger resigned his position as manager during the 1996-97 season being replaced by a former Poppies chairman Brian Talbot - his first game in total charge of the side recorded a 5-1 defeat of - guess who - Kettering Town, how ironic.

RUSSELL GLEN. Centre-back. Previous club: Corby Town. Glen's only league appearance for the club came as a second half substitute during the opening day of the 1992-93 campaign away at Slough Town. The Poppies lost 0-3 and Glen departed.

GM Vauxhall Conference, debut v Slough Town (a) 22:08:92
Appearances: 1   League 0+1   **Goals:** 0
                       Cups   0

RYAN PETER. Goalkeeper. Made his Poppies debut at the age of 16 against Barrow during the 1979-80 season. The poor lad conceded a goal in under 4 seconds* as Colin Cowperthwaite, (once the bane of Kettering), made it a nightmare start to Ryan's short Poppies career. A reserve keeper he made a second appearance in the 0-0 draw against Northwich Victoria, which at least erased his earlier outing 2 years prior. (* see quickest goal).

Alliance Premier League, debut v Barrow (h) 09:12:79

Appearances: 24   League 21
                          Cups   3

S

SADDINGTON JAMES. A Cambridge born Central defender - who originally started his career with Cambridge City later joining Millwall and then the Poppies on loan before his permanent move. Came to notice within 15 seconds of making his debut at Merthyr as probably the quickest booking for a debutee. Scored his only goal for the Poppies in the Northants Senior Cup final replay at Rockingham Road against Rushden & Diamonds, the game ending 2-2, the Poppies winning on penalties. Although James put in some impressive performances, he left the club during the 1995-96 season and rejoined Cambridge City, for a small fee.

GM Vauxhall Conference, debut v Merthyr Tydfil (a) 29:10:94

Appearances: 41   League 27+2   **Goals:** 1   League 0
Cups   9+3   Cups   1

SAMYORKE GABRIEL. Midfield. Previous club: Crawley Town. Made his debut for the club in the 0-5 defeat at Rothwell Town during the 1995-96 Northants Senior Cup semi-final and was never seen again.

Debut (County Cup) v Rothwell Town (a) 27:02:96

Appearances: 1   League 0   **Goals:** 0
Cups   1

SANDERCOCK PHIL. Full back. Born Plymouth. Previous clubs: Torquay United, Huddersfield Town, Northampton Town, Barnet and Weymouth. Joined Kettering in December 1983 from Weymouth. Phil's only goal for the club came in the 2-3 home defeat by Yeovil Town during the 1983-84 season.

Alliance Premier League, debut v Wealdstone (h) 26:12:83

Appearances: 25   League 22   **Goals:** 1   League 1
Cups   3

SANDEMAN BRADLEY. Full back. Born Northampton. Previoud clubs: Northampton Town, Maidstone United, Port Vale, Northwich Victoria and Stevenage Borough. Signed by Steve Berry in December 1997. Scored his first goal for the club at Rockingham Road in the 2-1 New Year's Day victory over Hednesford Town.

GM Vauxhall Conference, debut v Welling United (h) 13:12:97

Appearances: 28   League 24 **Goals:** 4   League 3
                        Cups   4   Cups   1

SCHIAVI MARK. Winger. Previous clubs: West Ham United and Northampton Town. While with the Hammers he represented England youth. An Alan Buckley signing during the 1987-88 close season. Made his league debut against the club he would later join, Enfield. After very few chances in the first team, Mark left the Poppies for Enfield during December - he would later score for his new club against the Poppies.

Debut (Maunsell Cup) v Northampton Town (h) 08:08:87
GM Vauxhall Conference, debut v Enfield (h) 22:08:87

Appearances: 21   League 11+4   **Goals:** 0
                        Cups   4+2

SCOPE DAVID*. Winger. Born Newcastle. Previous clubs: Blyth Spartans and Northampton Town. A loan signing made by Peter Morris from Northampton Town during the latter part of the 1989-90 season. Made his debut as a substitute in the 2-0 away victory at Yeovil Town, but his final game for the club was the 1-3 away defeat at the docklands against Fisher Athletic.

GM Vauxhall Conference, debut v Yeovil Town (a) 31:03:90

Appearances: 6   League 5+1   **Goals:** 0
                       Cups   0

SCORED AGAINST THE POPPIES. The following players have scored against the Poppies either before joining the club or since leaving the 'Temple of Science'. Carl Alford (Witton Albion, Rushden & Diamonds), Ian Arnold (Stalybridge Celtic), Stewart Atkins (Barnet), Glenn Beech (Boston United), Gary Butterworth (Rushden & Diamonds), Reckey Carter (Bromsgrove Rovers), Roy Clayton (Barnet & Corby Town), Glyn Creaser (Barnet), Paul Culpin (Nuneaton Borough), Warren Donald (Colchester United), Nicky Evans (Barnet), David Hofbauer (Corby Town), Steve Holden (Rushden & Diamonds), Junior Hunter (Woking), Gary Jones (Boston United), Ollie Kearns (Reading & Walsall), Bobby Mayes

(Redbridge Forest), Leroy May (Stafford Rangers), Frankie Murphy (Nuneaton Borough & Barnet), Matt Murphy (Corby Town), Micky Nuttell (Boston United, Rushden & Diamonds), Brian Palgrave (Solihull Borough), Brendan Phillips (Scarborough), Mark Schiavi (Enfield), Steve Stott (Bromsgrove Rovers, Rushden & Diamonds), Mark Whitehouse (Kidderminster Harriers).

SCOTT IAN. Forward. Born Leicester. Joined the Poppies at the end of the 1994-95 season from Hinckley Town for a £5,000 fee. Also a college student at Nottingham he made quite an impression not only with his early form but his acrobatic goal celebration that could have graced any Olympic floor show. Scotty struggled to maintain his form and lost confidence towards the latter part of the season. Ian joined the small band of outfield players that have played in goal for the club, deputising for Alan Judge who was sent off against Dagenham & Redbridge, the Poppies won 2-1, with Scotty being renamed, 'The Cat'. Joined Worcester City during the 1996-97 close season but opted for a move back to Hinckley a few months into the season.

Debut (County Cup) v Rushden & Diamonds (a) 27:07:95
GM Vauxhall Conference, debut v Altrincham (a) 19:08:95
Appearances: 55   League 30+8   **Goals:** 10 League 7
                        Cups   11+6   Cups   3

SELLERS JOHN. Midfield. Graduated from the Poppies youth policy, leaving for the 'Theatre of Dreams' at Old Trafford, Manchester, without a first team appearance for the Poppies. John returned to Rockingham Road in 1984 but after little opportunity in the first team joined Irthlingborough Diamonds during the 1986-87 pre-season.

Gola League, debut v Altrincham (a) 18:08:84
Appearances: 24   League 15+7   **Goals:** 0
                        Cups   1+1

SHANAHAN   JOHN.   Forward.   Previous   clubs: AFC Bournemouth (apprentice), Wealdstone and Edgeware. Made his debut during the 1995-96 Spalding Challenge Cup semi-final at Bromsgrove. Unfortunately after 40 minutes a late challenge on Reckey Carter, (who would later join the Poppies, briefly), and John was shown the red card. Made a couple of appearances in the Conference towards the end of the dismal 1995-96 season.

Debut (League Cup) v Bromsgrove Rovers (a) 19:03:96

124

GM Vauxhall Conference, debut v Telford United (h) 30:04:96
Appearances: 3   League 1+1   **Goals:** 0
Cups   1

SHAW STEPHEN. Central Defender. Youth team player who made his debut for the club as a second half substitute during the 0-5 away defeat at Rothwell in the 1995-96 Northants Senior Cup.
Debut (County Cup) v Rothwell Town (a) 27:02:96
Appearances: 1   League 0   **Goals:** 0
Cups   0+1

SHEARER MICK. Midfield. Signed during the 1992-93 season by Graham Carr from VS Rugby. Although he showed flashes of ability he could never sustain a constant place in a squad that boasted 53 players by the end of the campaign. Later played for Halesowen Town.
GM Vauxhall Conference, debut v Bath City (h) 20:02:93
Appearances: 5   League 3+1   **Goals:** 0
Cups   0+1

SHELTON CRAIG. Previous club: Leicester City. Made his Poppies debut at the age of 18 in midfield. Scored his first league goal in the 4-4 draw against Dartford at Rockingham Road in season 1981-82. The other league goal came in the same season against Weymouth, this time the Poppies lost 1-2 in front of their own fans.
Alliance Premier League, debut v AP Leamington (a) 07:11:81
Appearances: 39   League 25+5   **Goals:** 3   League 2
Cups   7+2   Cups   1

SHEPPARD SIMON. Goalkeeper. Born Clevedon. Previous clubs: Watford, Scarborough, Reading and Boreham Wood. The former England youth international was originally a trainee at Watford. Simon kicked off the 1995-96 season in goal for Reading before having a spell at Boreham Wood during the 1996-97 campaign. Simon never established himself during the dismal 1997-98 season and was released in December 1997, joining Hemel Hempstead after leaving the Poppies.
Debut (Maunsell Cup) v Northampton Town (h) 29:07:97
GM Vauxhall Conference, debut v Slough Town (h) 16:08:97
Appearances: 16   League 12
Cups   4

SHOEMAKE KEVIN. Goalkeeper. Born in Wickford. Previous clubs: Leyton Orient, Harlow, Chelmsford City (twice), Welling United, Peterborough United, Redbridge Forest, Rushden & Diamonds and Worcester City. The much travelled keeper has made probably more debuts for the club then any other player in the history of Kettering Town. Originally signed by Peter Morris during the 1988-89 close season. Kevin was backwards and forwards at the club with injury and disputes unsettling his run in the first teams.

Certainly without those two factors 'Shoey' would probably be in the top three all time goalkeepers appearance list. As it stands he is in 5th place with Gordon Livsey in pole position with 315 appearances. 'Shoey' was brought back by Gary Johnson during the 1995-96 close season as cover for Alan Judge. Nineteen minutes into Judge's debut against Altrincham our Kev was brought into action as Judgie was carried off. The Poppies went on to win 4-2. Shoey has always been a character, those of you that have stood behind his net will be able to testify. If injuries had been kind to this popular custodian I feel he would have played for the England non-league side, as it is he has served the Poppies proud. During the 1996-97 campaign he was knocked out twice and is one of the few keepers, with the exception of David Seaman, who has a better than 50% chance of saving a penalty. Kevin made 16 appearances during the season. Returned for the 1997-98 season where he made just 5, (4 in the FA Cup), appearances.

Debut (Maunsell Cup) v Peterborough United (h) 13:08:88
GM Vauxhall Conference, debut v Northwich Victoria (h) 20:08:88
Appearances: 157   League 115+4
                                    Cups   36+2

SHRIEVES TERRY. Born Ashford. Previous clubs: Woking, Hitchin, Milton Keynes and Buckingham. Joined the Poppies in October 1984. Scored his first goal for the club in the 4-3 victory against Enfield, scoring two more in the next game - the 6-1 win at Bath City. Unable to get a great deal of first team football under

Dave Needham and with Mark Smith and Keith Alexander pairing up in the forward line, Terry joined Aylesbury United during the 1985-86 season.

Gola League, debut v Telford United (a) 03:10:84

Appearances: 43   League 25+9   ***Goals:*** 15 League 10
                   Cups   6+3   Cups   5

SINDEN SVEN. Forward. Previous clubs: Shepshed Dynamo, Atherstone United, Hinckley United and Barwell. Had a spell as a trialist under Steve Berry's management, scoring on his debut in the Northants Senior Cup, a 1-0 home win against Wellingborough Town. Returned to Shepshed after making just a handful of appearances.

Debut (County Cup) v Wellingborough Town (h) 11:11:97
GM Vauxhall Conference, debut v Dover Athletic (h) 15:11:97

Appearances: 4   League 1+1   ***Goals:*** 1 League 0
                   Cups   2   Cups   1

SLACK TREVOR. Central defender. Born Peterborough. Previous clubs: Peterborough United, Rotherham United, Grimsby Town, Northampton Town, Barnet and Chesterfield. An excellent signing by Peter Morris, originally Trevor joined the Poppies on loan from Chesterfield due to an injury to Russell Lewis early on in the 1989-90 campaign. His career started under Morris at Peterborough United going on to make over 300 league appearances with a variety of clubs. Left Kettering under a cloud of mystery for Boston United during the 1992-93 close season.

GM Vauxhall Conference, debut v Enfield (a) 05:09:89

Appearances: 138   League 112+2   ***Goals:*** 9   League 8
                   Cups   24   Cups   1

SLAWSON STEVE. Forward. Born Nottingham. Previous clubs: Notts County and Rotherham United. A Steve Berry signing during the 1996-97 campaign. Steve scored his only goal for the club in the 1-0 away win at the Crabble, Dover, but was freed at the end of the season.

GM Vauxhall Conference debut v Northwich Victoria (a) 11:01:97

Appearances: 19   League 15+1   ***Goals:*** 1   League 1
                   Cups   3

SMALLEY MARK. Central defender. Born Newark. Previous clubs: Nottingham Forest, Birmingham City, Leyton Orient, Bristol

Rovers, Mansfield Town and Maidstone United. This former England Youth international was signed from Maidstone United by Graham Carr in October, during the 1992-93 season.

GM Vauxhall Conference, debut v Wycombe Wanderers (h) 26:09:92

Appearances: 24   League 18+1   **Goals:** 0
                           Cups   5

SMITH MARK*. Goalkeeper. Born Birmingham. Signed on loan during the 1993-94 season from Nottingham Forest. Saved a penalty against Boston United on his debut at Rockingham Road during the exciting 3-3 draw. Rejoined Forest after just one outing and later played for Crewe Alexandra, Walsall and Rushden Diamonds.

GM Vauxhall Conference, debut v Boston United (h) 28:12:92

Appearances: 1   League 1
                           Cups   0

SMITH MARK. Centre forward. Born Sheffield. Previous clubs: Sheffield United, Gainsborough Trinity, Worksop, Burton Albion and Buxton. A Dave Needham signing, Mark originally joined the Poppies in October 1984 from Buxton, scoring two goals against Boston United in the Poppies 2-1 win at Rockingham Road. One of only two Poppies players to score two goals on his debut - the other Marc North in 1991-92. Smithy left in the summer of 1985 and joined Shepshed Charterhouse. He rejoined Kettering in October 1985 but left the club during the 1988-89 close season to join Rochdale, (a major blow to all Poppies fans, as no doubt Mark was in the classic centre-forward mould), and a long football league career followed with a variety of clubs.

Gola League, debut v Boston United (h) 10:11:84

Appearances: 155   League 111+6   **Goals:** 62 League 44
                           Cups   37+1   Cups   18

SMITH PAUL*. Full back. Born Rotherham. Joined the Poppies on loan from Lincoln City during the 1994-95 season. Won the GMVC title with City in 1987-88. After his loan period expired he rejoined Lincoln. The following season he joined Halifax Town.

GM Vauxhall Conference, debut v Telford United (h) 15:10:94

Appearances: 11   League 8   **Goals:** 0
                           Cups   3

SMITH SCOTT. Defender. New Zealand under-21 international signed on free transfer just before the 1996-97 transfer deadline by Steve Berry on a non-contract basis from Rotherham United. Freed at the end of the campaign to Join Woking for the 1997-98 season.

GM Vauxhall Conference, debut v Welling United (a) 01:04:97

Appearances: 6   League 4+1   **Goals:** 0
Cups   1

SOMMER JURGEN*. Goalkeeper. Born New York (USA). Previous clubs: Luton Town, Brighton Hove Albion and Torquay United. Signed on loan from Luton during the 1992-93 season. An Arnerican who went on to establish himself at Luton before a big move to QPR in 1995. Will be remembered for his heroics at Wycombe Wanderers during our 2-1 away win and getting away with a blatant penalty decision in the 9th minute of injury time.

GM Vauxhall Conference, debut v Telford United (h) 02:02:93

Appearances: 12   League 10
Cups   2

SOWDEN SEAN. Utility. Born Blackburn. Previous clubs: Histon and Sheffield Wednesday. Signed by Dave Cusack during the summer of 1992 after his release from Sheffield Wednesday. Left not long after Cusack's departure, joining Sudbury Town.

GM Vauxhall Conference, debut v Slough Town (a) 22:08:92

Appearances: 7   League 6+1   **Goals:** 0
Cups   0

SPALDING CHALLENGE CUP. Another guise of the Bob Lord Trophy, this time sponsored by leading sports company Spalding. Their tenure of the competition started during the 1995-96 season, the Poppies reaching the semi-final stage, losing 3-2 on aggregate to Bromsgrove Rovers.

STEBBING GARY. Defender. Born Croydon. Signed after the demise of Maidstone United, by Graham Carr. Previous clubs, Crystal Palace, Southend United, KV Ostend (Belgium) and Maidstone United. After a short impressive stint with the Poppies, Gary disappointingly left for Dagenham & Redbridge, joining Dover Athletic after Dagenham's relegation in 1995-96.

GM Vauxhall Conference, debut v Macclesfield Town (a) 31:10:92

Appearances: 6   League 5   **Goals:** 0
Cups   0

STOCK RUSSELL. Forward. Born Great Yarmouth. A 1996-97 close season signing by Gary Johnson from his former club Cambridge United. Russell scored his first goal for the Poppies as a substitute against Welling United at Rockingham Road in only his second game for the club. Joined Sudbury Town on loan during February 1997 but returned to the Poppies towards the end of March. Russell was allowed to leave the club at the end of the season.

GM Vauxhall Conference, debut v Macclesfield Town (a) 17:08:96

Appearances: 28   League 14+6   **Goals:** 4   League 3
                      Cups   5+3   Cups   1

STOTT STEVE. Midfielder. Born Leeds. Joined the Poppies from Bromsgrove Rovers for a £12,500 fee during the 1995-96 close season. Steve's career with the Poppies only lasted four and a half months as Rushden & Diamonds bought him for £30,000 in an allegedly combined £100,000 attempt to lure striker Carl Alford to Nene Park. Stott left for pastures new, Alford remained for a while. Steve also played for Tranmere Rovers and Alvchurch before a lengthy career with Rovers. Scored his first goal for the club in the 4-0 home win against Runcorn. Later played for Yeovil Town.

Debut (County Cup) v Rushden & Diamonds (a) 27:07:95
GM Vauxhall Conference, debut v Altrincham (a) 19:08:95

Appearances: 27   League 18   **Goals:** 3   League 3
                      Cups   9

STRINGFELLOW IAN. Midfield. Born Nottingham Originally joined the Poppies on loan from Mansfield Town in 1992, but was recalled after just one appearance. Signed for the Club in 1994 from the Stags after making over 160 appearances including a Wembley Final in the Sherpa Van Trophy, where he scored in Mansfield's 5-4 penalty shoot out against Bristol City in 1987. Ian, the nephew of ex-Leicester City striker Mike, at times was brilliant but other times he faded away, which was not only frustrating to him but also the fans. Stringy started the 1995-96 season with 5 goals in 9 games but a combination of a full time college degree and constant travelling to training was too much and he moved to Vauxhall Conference rivals Dagenham & Redbridge at Christmas 1995. Linked up with Poppies boss Peter Morris at Kings Lynn.

GM Vauxhall Conference, debut v Gateshead (h) 28:11:92

Appearances: 92   League 60+8   **Goals:** 17   League 14
                      Cups   19+5   Cups   3

SUDDARDS SEAN. Central defender. Born Halifax. Previous club: Blackpool. A Ron Atkinson signing from the Seasiders in 1973. Known to the fans as 'Mr Dependable', one of the all time greats to feature at Rockingham Road. Sean holds the record of consecutive league matches played at 90. A class player who always seemed as cool as an ice berg during the thick of the action. Scored two of his goals in the Alliance Premier League Cup, one in 1979-80 at home v Weymouth, the Poppies winning 3-1 and 14 months later a strike against Barnet in the Poppies 4-1 3rd Round victory. A third goal came against Irthlingborough Diamonds in the Northants Senior Cup semi-final during the 1980-81 season. During the 1983-84 pre-season manager Jim Conde appointed Sean as player-coach. For outstanding service to the club Sean was awarded Testimonial matches against a star studded Manchester City side in 1980. 2,062 turned out to see City win 3-1. This was followed by the 1979 Poppies Wembley team v Derby County XI in 1982. The Poppies winning 4-3 in front of 1,300.

Southern Premier League, debut v Folkestone (h) 11:08:73
Alliance Premier League, debut v Stafford Rangers (a) 18:08:79

Appearances: 150   League 118   **Goals:** 4   League 0
Cups   32   Cups   4

SULLIVAN ROBERT. Full back. A Peter Morris signing from Peterborough United during the 1989-90 season whose only appearance for the club came in the Northants Senior Cup semi-final against Brackley Town, the Poppies winning 2-1.

Debut (County Cup) v Brackley Town (a) 06:03:90

Appearances: 1   League 0   **Goals:** 0
Cups   1

SWAILES CHRIS. Central defender. Born Gateshead. Previous clubs: Ipswich Town, Peterborough United, Birmingham City, Boston United and Doncaster Rovers. Signed by Dave Cusack during the 1992-93 close season from Boston. Left the Poppies after only a handful of games and joined Bridlington.

Debut (Maunsell Cup) v Peterborough United (h) 08:08:92
GM Vauxhall Conference, debut v Slough Town (a) 22:08:92

Appearances: 6   League 3+2   **Goals:** 0
Cups   1

T

TALLENTIRE DEAN. Central defender signed by Steve Berry from Northampton Town just before the transfer deadline towards the latter part of the 1996-97 season.

GM Vauxhall Conference, debut v Altrincham (a) 26:04:97

Appearances: 2   League 2   **Goals:** 0

Cups   0

TAYLOR CHRIS. Goalkeeper. Born Birmingham. Previous clubs: Cheltenham Town, Bromsgrove Rovers, Halesowen Town, Evesham United, Moor Green and Solihull Borough. Signed by Steve Berry in November 1997. As soon as Chris signed for the club results improved. It just goes to show you that with a competent goalkeeper behind a sticky defence players have more confidence. Chris played an important part in keeping the club in the top flight of non-league football with a series of impressive performances. But when Steve Berry left the club he joined the mass exodus of players leaving the Poppies for rivals Stevenage Borough during the 1998-99 close season.

GM Vauxhall Conference, debut v Rushden & Diamonds (a) 25:11:97

Appearances: 31   League 27

Cups   4

TAYLOR ROBIN. A stylish midfielder signed originally from Shepshed Albion during the 1992-93 season by Graham Carr but made such a good impression after two games he was bound for Peterborough United before returning in 1993-94. Left the Poppies due to increasing work commitments but resurrected his playing career under his former manager Graham Carr at Dagenham & Redbridge. While at Loughborough University he represented the British Students at the World Games in the USA. Went on to play for Woking.

GM Vauxhall Conference, debut v Bromsgrove Rovers (a) 23:01:93

Appearances: 83   League 67+2   *Goals:* 9   League 9
Cups   14

TELEVISION. Kettering Town Football Club have featured on the BBC's Match of the Day in highlights of various FA Cup encounters: Bristol Rovers, Halifax, Maidstone United, Charlton Athletic, Blackburn and Gillingham to name but a few. Local coverage is generally more prominent when either the club is having a good FA Cup, FA Trophy run, are top of the League or when the club is in financial difficulties, or in the winding up process! It is rare the club is covered by BBC Midlands, East, Central or Anglia TV during a normal sporting weekend. The one highlight was during the 1994-95 FA Cup campaign when *SKY Sports* decided to air the FA 1st Round tie, Kettering Town v Plymouth Argyle, from Rockingham Road. The first football club in the county to have a live match staged nationally from their ground. The Poppies lost 0-1. Kettering also featured in a handful of games on the now defunct Sportscast (British Aerospace) and Wire TV cable services.

THACKER TIM. Full back. Born Nottingham. Previous clubs: Notts County, Grantham and Shepshed Charterhouse. Joined the Poppies during the summer of 1984. Another player whose impressive performances were rewarded by being voted Player of the Year for season 1985-86. A no nonsense full back who always gave 100%, a Poppies fans favourite. Unfortunately his career came to a tragic end during the FA Cup 1st Qualifying Round against Lowerstoft. A collision with Kettering goalkeeper Mark Harrison in the second half, ending up with a broken leg - his last appearance for the club, a player sadly missed by many. Tim was awarded a benefit match against a Leicester City side in 1988. 1,235 turned out to watch the Foxes win 2- 0.
Debut (Maunsell Cup) v Peterborough United (h) 15:08:84
Gola League, debut v Altrincham (a) 18:08:84
Appearances: 109   League 84   *Goals:* 2   League
Cups   25

THOMAS ANTON. Striker. Born Northampton. Joined the club from local rivals Corby Town in the 1994-95 close season. Anton played for the Poppies nursery side, Kettering FC in 1986 but went on to play for Bedworth, Leicester United and a period in Malta before joining the Steelmen. He made an impression during his first season with the club, but an injury sustained during the pre-season in 1995-96 ruled him out of the frame for eight months. Came back to score the winning goal at Dagenham & Redbridge towards the end of the season, but injury again ruled him out of the final few games. Anton left the Poppies during the 1996-97 close season for Worcester City.

GM Vauxhall Conference, debut v Runcorn (a) 20:08:94

Appearances: 59   League 35+7   **Goals:** 14 League 9
                       Cups   13+3   Cups   5

THORBON LES. Goalkeeper. A Don Masson signing during the 1983-84 close season from Wellingborough Town, primarily as a reserve keeper.   Made his solitary appearance in the Northants Senior Cup semi-final against Corby Town, Poppies winning 4-1.

Debut (County Cup) v Corby Town (h) 17:03:84

Appearances: 1   League 0
                       Cups   1

THORPE ADRIAN. Winger. Born Chesterfield. Previous clubs: Heanor Town, Bradford City, Tranmere Rovers, Notts County and Northampton Town. A speedy winger signed by Graham Carr during the 1993-94 season. Plenty of experience who only played part of a season with the Poppies, leaving Kettering to pursue a career in the Fire Service. Later played for Arnold Town.

Debut (Maunsell Cup) v Northampton Town (h) 07:08:93
GM Vauxhall Conference, debut v Witton Albion (h) 30.08:93

Appearances: 17   League 8+4   **Goals:** 4 League 2
                       Cups   4+1   Cups   2

THROWER NIGEL. Full back. Born Nottingham. Previous clubs: Shepshed Charterhouse, Nottingham Forest and Chesterfield. A Dave Needham signing during the 1984-85 close season from Shepshed. Nigel's only goal for the club came in the 4-1 home win against Gateshead during the 1984-85 season.

Debut (Maunsell Cup) v Peterborough United (h) 15:08:84
Gola League, debut v Altrincham (a) 18:08:84

Appearances: 49   League 38 **Goals:** 1 League 1
                       Cups   11

TILLSON ANDY. Huntingdon born central defender whose previous club was Stamford. Andy joined the Poppies from the Lincolnshire side in August 1986.   He was allowed to join

134

Peterborough United but re-signed during the 1987-88 season. Whilst at Kettering it was obvious that his stay was going to be a short one. The Rockingham Road faithful never really saw the best of Andy and he left for Grimsby Town, later QPR then Bristol Rovers.

GM Vauxhall Conference, debut v Weymouth (a) 16:08:86

Appearances: 37   League 30 **Goals:** 3   League 3
Cups   7

TINGAY PHIL. Goalkeeper. Born Chesterfield. Previous clubs: Chesterfield, Barnsley and Lincoln City. Joined the Poppies in October 1981 from Chesterfield and took over the goalkeepers shirt from Kevin Fox.

Alliance Premier League, debut v Gravesend & Northfleet (h) 10:10:81

Appearances: 49   League 37
Cups   1

TOMLINSON DAVID. Previous clubs: Rotherham United, York City, Gainsborough Trinity, Boston United and Barnet. Winger signed by Dave Cusack from Barnet during the 1992-93 close season in exchange for Richard Huxford. David's only goal for the club was an equalising effort against Farnborough Town, a game the Poppies went on to win 2-1. Later moved to Matlock Town.

Debut (Maunsell Cup) v Peterborough United (h) 08:08:92
GM Vauxhall Conference, debut v Slough Town (a) 22:08:92

Appearances: 9   League 5+3   **Goals:** 1   League 1
Cups   1

TORRANCE GARY. Midfield. Born Corby. A Peter Morris signing during the 1988-89 close season after being released from Leicester City. Made two appearances for the club but only one start in the 0-1 away defeat at Brackley Town in the NSC semi-final.

Debut (Maunsell Cup) v Peterborough United (h) 13:08:88

Appearances: 2   League 0   **Goals:** 0
Cups   1+1

TORRANCE NEIL. Goalkeeper whose only appearance for the Poppies was against Cheltenham Town in the 1-5 Gola League thrashing at Whadden Road during the 1985-86 campaign.

Gola League, debut v Cheltenham Town (a) 19:10:85

Appearances: 1   League 1
Cups   0

TRANSFERS. Andy Hunt holds the club record after his transfer for £150,000 to Newcastle United during 1990-91, while Carl Alford holds the record price paid out by the club, £25,000 from Macclesfield Town during the 1994-95 close season. Although the club shelled out a combined £26,000 fee for Reckey Carter and Craig Gaunt from Bromsgrove Rovers during the 1996-97 close season.

TRANSFER LIST:

Out going. Transfer records:

£150,000	-	Andy Hunt to Newcastle United.
£85,000	-	Carl Alford to Rushden & Diamonds.
£60,000	-	Cohen Griffiths to Cardiff City.
£30,000	-	Steve Stott to Rushden & Diamonds.
£25,000	-	Kofi Nyamah to Stoke City.
£17,500	-	Reckey Carter to Solihull Borough.
£15,000	-	Richard Brown to Blackburn Rovers.
£15,000	-	Ian Arnold to Stalybridge Celtic.
£14,000	-	Nick Ashby to Rushden & Diamonds.
£14,000	-	Chris Pearson to Stevenage Borough.
£10,000	-	Frank Murphy to Barnet.
£10,000	-	Les Lawrence to Aylesbury United.
£10,000	-	Paul Reece to Grimsby Town.

Incoming. Transfer records:

£25,000	-	Carl Alford from Macclesfield Town.
£20,000	-	Reckey Carter from Bromsgrove Rovers.
£17,500	-	Gary Jones from Grantham.
£12,500	-	Steve Stott from Bromsgrove Rovers.
£10,000	-	Ian Arnold from Carlisle United.
£10,000*	-	Leroy May from Kidderminster Harriers.

*Would have risen to £15,000 after 25-50 appearances for the club, but never materialised.

TRIGG SIMON*. Forward who was signed by Gary Johnson during the 1995-96 season. Simon had been on West Bromwich Albion's books. On leaving the Poppies after a handful of unimpressive games he joined Raunds Town and later played for Corby Town.

Debut (FA Cup) v Bromsgrove Rovers (a) 24:10:95

GM Vauxhall Conference, debut v Dagenham & Redbridge (h) 04:11:95
Appearances: 7   League 1+2   **Goals:** 0
                       Cups   3+1

TRINDER JASON*. Goalkeeper. Born Leicester. Signed on loan from Grimsby Town during the 1993-94 season. Played one game in the BLT against Welling United and within 25 seconds Terry Robbins had put the ball past the youngster before he even had chance to touch the spherical object. Welling won the tie 2-1 at the Park View Stadium.

Debut (League Cup) v Welling United (a) 21:09:93
Appearances: 1   League 0
                       Cups   1

TURLEY BILLY*. Goalkeeper. Born Wolverhampton. Previous clubs: Northampton Town and Evesham. Signed on loan from Northampton Town by Steve Berry during the 1996-97 season. Billy came into the side just as the Poppies produced their best form of the season, impressive performances from the Northampton man, accumulated with a great penalty save in the 3-1 home win over Kidderminster Harriers before a recall to the Cobblers on the eve of the long awaited local derby v Rushden & Diamonds. During Billy's first stint between the sticks the Poppies did not lose a game while only conceeding four goals. Returned for a second period on loan just before the transfer deadline. Later played for Leyton Orient.

Debut (County Cup) v Cogenhoe United (h) 21:01:97
GM Vauxhall Conference debut v Bath City (h) 25:01:97
Appearances: 10   League 8
                        Cups   1

TURNER IAN. Midfield. Joined the Poppies from Burton Albion during the 1984-85 close season. Made his only Gola League start against Runcorn in the 2-2 draw at Canal Street.

Gola League, debut v Altrincham (a) 18:08:84
Appearances: 11   League 1+6   **Goals:** 0
                        Cups   1+3

U

UNDERWOOD SIMON. Forward. Signed by Dave Cusack during the summer of 1992 after completing his apprenticeship at Northampton Town. Simon made his debut as a substitute against Farnborough Town during the 2-1 win at Rockingham Road.

GM Vauxhall Conference, debut v Farnborough Town (h) 08:09:92

Appearances: 1   League 0 + 1   **Goals:** 0
                                Cups   0

Simon's one appearance for the Poppies made him the fourth Underwood (not related), the first in 1911, to play for Kettering and one of only six players whose name begins with the letter U.

V

VAN DULLEMAN RAYMOND*: Forward. Previous club: Northampton Town. A Steve Berry signing on loan from Northampton Town during 1997 - the first Dutchman to play for the club. Scored his first goal for the Poppies in the 1-1 home draw against then leaders Halifax Town and his second in the 7-1 thrashing of Long Buckby in the Northants Hillier Senior Cup semi-final. After a three month loan period the popular forward returned to Northampton Town.

GM Vauxhall Conference, debut v Morecambe (a) 20:12:97

Appearances: 12   League 10+1   **Goals:** 2   League 1
                       Cups   1   Cups   1

VENABLES DAVE. Forward. Born Horsham. Previous clubs: Eastbourne United, Wealdstone, Crawley Town and Stevenage Borough. A Steve Berry signing for £9,000 from former club Stevenage Borough during the 1996-97 campaign. Dave was a member of the Stevenage side that won the 1995-96 GMVC title. Scored his first and only goal for Kettering in the Poppies 3-1 win over Farnborough Town but broke his ankle against Stalybridge Celtic in March and this curtailed his 1996-97 appearances. After a disappointing start to the 1997-98 season and with the club in financial difficulties, Dave was sold to Enfield in September for £5,000.

GM Vauxhall Conference, debut v Hayes (a) 21:12:96

Appearances: 19   League 13+3   **Goals:** 1   League 1
                       Cups   3

VINTER MICK. Striker. Previous clubs: Wrexham and Notts County. A Peter Morris signing in 1987-88 he scored his only goal for the Poppies on his debut as a substitute in the 1-2 defeat against Altrincham becoming the first of only three players to score on their debuts as a substitute.

Appearances: 2   League 0+2   ***Goals:*** 1   League 1
                     Cups   0

VICTORIES. The Poppies record league win is by five clear goals, this feat has been achieved on seven occasions. For the record; 6-1 v Frickley Athletic - 1980-81, 6-1 v Bath City & 5-0 v Frickley Athletic - 1984-85, 5-0 v Dagenham - 1987-88, 5-0 v Boston United - 1988-89, 5-0 v Altrincham - 1991-92, 5-0 v Slough Town - 1992-93.

Also 6-1 v Atherstone United (FA Cup 2nd Qualifying Round) - 1996-97.

The most league victories by the Poppies, 23 on two occasions - 1988-89 & 1990-91. The most league victories at Rockingham Road, 16 in 1988-89 and the most league away victories, 11 in 1990-91. The fewest league victories, just 9 in 1981-82. Consecutive league victories, 7 in 1990-91.

VOWDEN COLIN. Centre-back. Born Newmarket. Previous clubs: Newmarket, Cambridge City and Cambridge United. A Steve Berry signing on a free transfer from Cambridge United during the 1997-98 close season. An impressive asset during a difficult campaign. Colin came through with flying colours winning the prestigious, 'Supporters' Player of the Season', award for his outstanding season with the club. Colin scored his first Conference goal for the Poppies in the 1-3 home defeat by Telford United.

Debut (Maunsell Cup) v Northampton Town (h) 29:07:97
GM Vauxhall Conference, debut v Slough Town (h) 16:08:97

Appearances: 52   League 38+2   ***Goals:*** 6   League 5
                     Cups   10+2   Cups   1

Only three other first team players throughout the history books have a surname beginning with the letter 'V' they are, Ronald Viner (1924-25), PA Vials (1926-27), Geoff Vowden (1974-75).

W

WADDICOR JOHN. Utility. Made his Alliance debut during the final three games of the 1982-83 season, the first as a substitute at Rockingham Road in the Poppies 5-2 win over Yeovil Town.
Alliance Premier League, debut v Yeovil Town (h) 30:04:83
Appearances: 4   League 1+2   **Goals:** 0
Cups   1

WALKER RICHARD*. Central defender. Born Derby. Richard was signed on loan from Notts County by Peter Morris during the 1991-92 season and scored his only and debut goal against Witton Albion in the 1-1 draw at Rockingham Road.
GM Vauxhall Conference, debut v Witton Albion (h) 31:08:91
Appearances: 6   League 5+1   **Goals:** 1   League 1
Cups   0

WALLER DAVE*. Forward. Born Urmston.   Previous clubs: Crewe Alexandra, Shrewsbury Town and Chesterfield. Signed by Peter Morris on loan from Chesterfield during the 1991-92 season. Made a cup appearance during the now famous 1-4 FA Cup 3rd Round away defeat at Ewood Park, Blackburn.
GM Vauxhall Conference, debut v Boston United (a) 26:12:91
Appearances: 8   League 2+4   **Goals:** 0
Cups   1+1

WALSH MARIO*. Striker. Born London. Previous clubs: Portsmouth, Torquay, Southend United and Colchester United. Signed on loan by Peter Morris from Colchester United during the early part of the 1991-92 season. Failed to impress and went back to Colchester.
GM Vauxhall Conference, debut v Kidderminster Harriers (h) 21:08:91.
Appearances: 5   League 5   **Goals:** 0
Cups   0

WALES. Only centre-back Russell Lewis has represented the Welsh semi-professional side whilst playing for Kettering since 1979.

WALTERS PETER. Goalkeeper. Previous clubs: Bedford and Corby Town. Signed for the Poppies during the 1980 close season for £500 from Bedford. An impressive keeper who commanded the six yard box with pride. Played in every game for the Poppies during the 1980-81 season. Left the club due to work commitments. Later played for Scarborough.

Alliance Premier League, debut v Worcester City (a) 16:08:80
Appearances: 53   League 38
                         Cups   15

WALWYN KEITH. Jamaican born. The experienced striker was signed by Peter Morris from Carlisle United during the 1990-91 season. Previous clubs, Winterton Rangers, Chesterfield, York City, Blackpool and Carlisle United. Both of Keith's cup goals came in the 3-2 defeat by Emley in the FA Trophy 3rd Round. Unfortunately he suffered a mild heart attack during a league game against Altrincham at Rockingham Road, which effectively ended his playing career.

GM Vauxhall Conference, debut v Cheltenham Town (a) 16:02:91
Appearances: 10   League 7   **Goals:** 3   League 1
                         Cups   3   Cups   2

WARD STEVE. Full back. Born Derby. Previous clubs: Brighton Hove Albion, Northampton Town and Halifax Town. Steve joined the Poppies during the summer of 1986 and could play in either the right or left back position and on occasions he also played in midfield. Steve scored his first goal for the club against Northwich Victoria in the Poppies 3-1 win.

GM Vauxhall Conference, debut v Weymouth (a) 16:08:86
Appearances: 101   League 75+2   **Goals:** 3   League 2
                          Cups   24   Cups   1

WATSON DAVE. Central defender. Previous clubs: Notts County (twice), Rotherham United, Sunderland, Manchester City, Southampton, Stoke City, Derby County, Werder Bremen (Germany) and Vancouver Whitecaps (Canada), also an England International. Won the FA Cup with Sunderland in 1973 and

142

League Cup with Manchester City in 1975-76. Dave was signed during an injury crisis facing Dave Needham. Came out of retirement for the 1985-86 campaign. Scored on his home debut against Northwich Victoria the 2-1 win and followed that up with another goal five days later in the 3-0 away win at Nuneaton Borough. His final goal for the club was at Bucks Head, Telford in the Poppies 2-2 draw. Retired at the end of the season.

Gola League debut v Altrincham (a) 24:08:85

Appearances: 14 League 10 **Goals:** 3 League 3
Cups 4

WHARTON DAVE. Central defender. Born Chesterfield. Previous clubs: Eastwood Town and Shepshed Charterhouse. Dave had trials with Liverpool and Chesterfield, but his career started at little Eastwood Town. He joined Kettering from Shepshed during the 1984-85 close season. Dave's impressive performances during the 1984-85 season were rewarded by being voted as Player of the Season. Dave scored his first Gola goal at the International Stadium Gateshead in the Poppies 4-1 victory. He was allowed to move to Stafford Rangers during January 1987 by Alan Buckley.

Debut (Maunsell Cup) v Peterborough United (h) 15:08:84
Gola League debut v Altrincham (a) 18:08:84

Appearances: 130 League 96+3 **Goals:** 4 League 4
Cups 31

WHITEHOUSE MARK*. Striker. Born Birmingham. Previous clubs: Bromsgrove Rovers, Kidderminster Harriers, Burton Albion, Worcester City, Redditch United, Tamworth, Oldbury and Moor Green. A Graham Carr signing towards the end of the 1993-94 campaign. Scored two spectacular goals both away from home, a magical equaliser against Northwich and a 25 yard volley at Southport. But even such a prolific striker as Mark couldn't inspire the side as the Poppies finished runners-up three points behind Kidderminster Harriers for the Vauxhall Conference Championship.

GM Vauxhall Conference debut v Merthyr Tydfil (a) 02:04:94

Appearances: 6 League 6 **Goals:** 2 League 2
Cups 2

WHITEHURST BILLY. Centre-forward. Born Thurnscoe. Previous clubs: Mexborough, Hull City (twice), Newcastle United, Oxford United, Reading, Sunderland, Sheffield United, Stoke City, Doncaster Rovers and Crewe Alexandra. The experienced, powerful and well travelled striker signed by Graham Carr during the 1992-93 season, but left the club soon after due to injury.

GM Vauxhall Conference, debut v Northwich Victoria (a) 19:09:92

Appearances: 4   League 3+1   **Goals:** 0
Cups   0

WILKES TIM. Forward. Born Nottingham. Previous club, Notts County. A 19 year old signed by Steve Berry during the latter stages of the 1996-97 season. Tim appeared in the Notts County first team twice before coming to Kettering. Scored his first goal for the club in the 1-0 home win over Northwich Victoria. Made much more of an impact during the following season ending up just one goal behind Chris Pearson as the club's leading scorer. Scored both goals in the 2-1 Senior Cup Final win over Raunds Town

GM Vauxhall Conference debut v Telford United (h) 15:03:97

Appearances: 60   League 32+15   **Goals:** 15 League 9
Cups   9+4   Cups   6

WOOD GARY. Full back. Born Kettering. Previous club: Notts County. Joined Kettering from Notts County in February 1983. Made his Alliance debut in the 1-3 home defeat by Wealdstone, the third in a nine game run without a league win. Gary was released by Don Masson during the 1983- 84 close season.

Alliance Premier League, debut v Wealdstone (h) 19:02:83

Appearances: 14   League 14   **Goals:** 0
Cups   0

WOOD IAN. Defender. Born Kirkby in Ashfield. Previous clubs: Mansfield Town, Aldershot, Boston United, Wellingborough Town and Kings Lynn. Ian joined the Poppies from Kings Lynn during the Linnetts staff cutting exercise in October 1985. A well seasoned professional who was voted Players Player of the Year for season 1985-86. Ian made his debut in the 0-0 draw at Maidstone and had to wait until the following season to score his first Vauxhall Conference goal in the 3-0 home win over Weymouth. Scored his other two goals in the 2-2 draw against Stafford Rangers at Rockingham Road. Released by Alan Buckley joining Corby Town during the 1987-88 close season.

Debut (Maunsell Cup) v Northampton Town (h) 30:10:88
Gola League, debut v Maidstone United (a) 02:11:85

Appearances: 77   League 54   **Goals:** 3   League 3
Cups   23

WOODS SHAUN. Midfielder signed by Graham Carr during the 1992-93 season from Leicestershire Senior League club St Andrews. Shaun scored his only goal for the Poppies in the 2-0 home win against Gateshead. Left the club the following pre-season and joined Leicester St Andrews.

GM Vauxhall Conference, debut v Kidderminster Harriers (a) 19:10:92
Appearances: 32   League 25+1   **Goals:** 1   League 1
                 Cups   5+1

WOODSFORD JAMIE*. Forward. Born Ipswich. Previous clubs: Luton Town and Portadown (Ireland). Signed by Gary Johnson on loan from Luton Town early into the 1996-97 campaign. Scored on his debut in the 1-1 draw at Slough Town before returning to Luton a few games later. Played for Hitchin on loan later the same season.

GM Vauxhall Conference, debut v Slough Town (a) 24:09:96
Appearances: 4   League 3   **Goals:** 1   League 1
                 Cups   1

WRIGHT ANDY. Born Kettering. Previous clubs: Desborough Town and Rothwell Town. First played for the Poppies as a 17 year old during the troubled 1981-82 season. A reliable defender who once appeared on the TV Quiz show the 'Krypton Factor'. Rejoined the Poppies in 1988 and made the majority of his appearances under Peter Morris, becoming almost a mainstay in the team. Developed the long throw in as a specialist trick which often resulted in a goal when hurled into the penalty area. Once scored three goals in two games during the 1982-83 season but ended up on the losing side both times. He also scored two goals against Kidderminster Harriers, one in the 1-1 away draw in 1988-89 and the winner at Aggborough during the 1989-90 campaign as the Poppies ran out 3-2 victors. Andy's final Conference goal was in the 2-0 home win over Sutton United, the final Saturday of the 1989-90 season. Left the Poppies during the 1990-91 season for Aylesbury United.

Alliance Premier League, debut v Bath City (h) 06:02:81
Appearances: 100   League 61+17   **Goals:** 11   League 7
                   Cups   21+1   Cups   4

WRIGHT OWEN. Winger. Previous clubs: Shepshed Albion, Worcester City, Bedworth United, Shepshed Charterhouse,

Rothwell Town and Aylesbury United. A Graham Carr signing during the 1992-93 season from Shepshed Albion. A promising talent who shone periodically. He was in outstanding form against Wycombe Wanderers during the Poppies 2-1 win at Adams Park, but these performances were very few and far between. Owen's only Conference goal came in injury time at Welling United, as the Poppies came back to draw 1-1. He was released at the end of 1994-95 season and later played a few games for Nuneaton Borough, Knighton Athletic and Corby Town.

GM Vauxhall Conference, debut v Boston United (h) 28:12:92

Appearances: 73   League 46+12   **Goals:** 4   League 1
                    Cups   11+4   Cups 3

X

X-FILES. Who were those players ? The truth is out there! There have been a host of players either training with or trying to impress, the various Poppies managers over the years. Three that I picked out of the bag are, Mark Heeley, a flying winger who joined the club (briefly) in October 1985 after previously playing for Peterborough United, Arsenal, Northampton Town, Aylesbury United, Stamford and Buckingham Town. Mark soon departed, although he did appear in a couple of the pen pictures in away programmes but he never featured for the club on the field. Goalkeeper Paul Warnecki joined the Poppies during 1986 as emergency cover but never donned the green jersey, after previously playing for Wolverton Town and Buckingham Town - later played for Irthlingborough Diamonds. Finally, forward Simon Guthrie, signed by Graham Carr from Gateshead during the 1993-94 close season remained a mystery. He scored a great goal against Port Vale in a pre-season friendly getting injured later in the same game. Simon was never seen in the Poppy red or stripey shirt again, just disappearing from Rockingham Road life. Was he abducted by aliens, did he fly over the Corby Triangle or pass into another dimension through a worm hole? My own theory is, his leg injury couldn't be repaired sufficiently to resurrect his playing career and he was quietly released after his rehabilitation programme.

XMAS MATCHES. The time of the derby matches! The Poppies have faced Boston United, Telford United, Stevenage Borough, Hednesford Town and Dagenham & Redbridge all supposed derby matches on Boxing Day. The real local derby should have begun when Rushden & Diamonds entered the fray in 1996-97. The game on Boxing Day at Rockingham Road and the return leg on New Years Day at Nene Park were victims of the weather. Both matches were played in March with the Diamonds inflicting a heavy

1-5 defeat at Rockingham Road and 10 days later a fortunate 1-0 win at Nene Park to complete the double over the Poppies.

The Boston United fixture evoked rivalry and passion with large attendances following both fixtures but none matched the 4,628 at Rockingham Road, (the highest league gate since the Colchester United fixture during the 1990-91 season), v Rushden & Diamonds and 5,170 at Nene Park for the return fixture, a club record.

Y

YORK PAUL. A Dave Needham 1986-87 pre-season signing from Irthlingborough Diamonds. Paul found life at Rockingham Road difficult, being unable to sustain a first team berth regularly. Made his first appearance as a substitute during the Poppies worst ever Conference result, the 0-8 defeat at Gander Green, Sutton, hardly the best way to start your career. Paul left the club for Aylesbury United.

GM Vauxhall Conference, debut v Sutton United (a) 14:10:86

Appearances: 5   League 2+1   **Goals:** 0

Cups   1+1

YOUNGEST PLAYERS. Many players have played for the club in their teens but Lawrie Dudfield and Peter Ryan both aged 16 hold the tag as the youngest players to have pulled on a Poppies jersey. Both played for the first team in a first class fixture.

Z

Zero points from a possible 24, the worst run in the club's history, (formed in 1872), was unfortunately recorded during the last eight GM Vauxhall Conference league games of the 1995-96 season. This overlapped to zero points from a possible 30 and ten games when Gary Johnson's team continued their losing streak into the 1996-97 season. The sequence was finally ended on August 24th 1996, when goals from Neil Pope and Tarkan Mustafa sent Bath City crashing 2-0 at Twerton Park.

Zero league wins in thirteen Conference matches - a record - at the onset of the 1997-98 season and was finally ended with a 2-1 home win over Dover Athletic on November 15th.

For the record Kettering actually went 17 league matches without a win stretching back to the 2-1 win at Welling, March 31st 1997.

STATISTICS

1979-98

KETTERING TOWN

LEAGUE STATISTICS
1979-80 TO 1997-98

OPPONENTS	P	HOME					AWAY					COMBINED				
		W	D	L	F	A	W	D	L	F	A	W	D	L	F	A
ALTRINCHAM	36	7	6	5	35	26	3	7	8	27	37	10	13	13	62	63
AP LEAMINGTON	6	1	1	1	5	3	1	2	0	9	7	2	3	1	14	10
AYLESBURY UNITED	2	1	0	0	5	2	1	0	0	1	0	2	0	0	6	2
BANGOR CITY	8	1	0	3	7	9	1	1	2	5	8	2	1	5	12	17
BARNET	24	7	3	2	25	14	6	0	6	18	23	13	3	8	43	37
BARROW	18	5	1	3	14	12	3	1	5	7	14	8	2	8	21	26
BATH CITY	32	5	6	5	21	17	4	6	6	23	23	9	12	11	44	40
BOSTON UNITED	28	7	4	3	28	16	4	2	8	17	25	11	6	11	45	41
BROMSGROVE ROVERS	10	2	1	2	7	6	3	1	1	13	7	5	2	3	20	13
CHELTENHAM TOWN	16	5	2	1	14	4	2	2	4	11	16	7	4	5	25	20
CHORLEY	4	2	0	0	5	1	1	1	0	3	2	3	1	0	8	3
COLCHESTER UNITED	4	1	1	0	3	2	0	0	2	2	6	1	1	2	5	8
DAGENHAM	14	3	1	3	12	9	3	0	4	12	10	6	1	7	24	19
DAGENHAM & REDBRIDGE	8	1	3	0	5	3	3	0	1	8	6	4	3	1	13	9
DARLINGTON	2	0	0	1	1	3	0	0	1	1	2	0	0	2	2	5
DARTFORD	6	0	2	1	6	8	2	1	0	5	2	2	3	1	11	10
DOVER ATHLETIC	10	3	2	0	7	4	3	1	1	5	2	6	3	1	12	6
ENFIELD	18	6	0	3	14	11	1	5	3	13	17	7	5	6	27	28
FARNBOROUGH TOWN	14	4	1	2	13	9	2	3	2	11	9	6	4	4	24	18
FISHER ATHLETIC	8	4	0	0	10	4	0	2	2	2	7	4	2	2	12	11
FRICKLEY ATHLETIC	14	4	1	2	18	5	0	3	4	8	16	4	4	6	26	21
GATESHEAD	22	7	3	1	23	8	3	7	1	12	9	10	10	2	35	17
GRAVESEND & NORTHFLEET	6	2	1	0	4	1	1	1	1	5	4	3	2	1	9	5
HALIFAX TOWN	10	2	1	2	11	6	0	1	4	2	9	2	1	6	13	15
HAYES	4	0	2	0	3	3	1	0	1	2	2	1	2	1	5	5
HEDNESFORD TOWN	6	2	0	1	4	3	0	2	1	1	2	2	2	2	5	5
HEREFORD UNITED	2	0	0	1	1	2	0	0	1	2	3	0	0	2	3	5
KIDDERMINSTER HARRIERS	30	6	6	3	26	20	4	4	7	18	27	10	10	10	44	47
LEEK TOWN	2	1	0	0	1	0	1	0	0	4	0	2	0	0	5	0
LINCOLN CITY	2	1	0	0	2	0	1	0	0	1	0	2	0	0	3	0
MACCLESFIELD TOWN	20	6	2	2	13	9	3	3	4	7	9	9	5	6	20	18
MAIDSTONE UNITED	20	3	3	4	15	15	3	2	5	9	18	6	5	9	24	33
MORECAMBE	6	0	1	2	3	6	1	0	2	8	11	1	1	4	11	17
MERTHRL TYDFILL	12	4	1	1	12	5	2	0	4	9	12	6	1	5	21	17
NEWPORT COUNTY	1	-	-	-	-	-	-1	0	0	2	1	1	0	0	2	1
NORTHWICH VICTORIA	38	11	6	2	30	23	3	9	7	22	33	14	15	9	52	55
NUNEATON BOROUGH	14	1	4	2	11	12	2	4	1	11	5	3	8	3	22	17
REDBRIDGE FOREST	2	1	0	0	3	2	0	0	1	0	4	1	0	1	3	6
REDDITCH UNITED	2	1	0	0	2	1	1	0	0	1	0	2	0	0	3	1
RUNCORN	30	8	6	1	29	11	2	4	9	15	31	10	10	10	44	42
RUSHDEN & DIAMONDS	4	0	0	2	1	9	0	0	2	0	2	0	0	4	1	11
SCARBOROUGH	16	2	2	4	8	10	2	2	4	5	10	4	4	8	13	20
SLOUGH TOWN	14	3	3	1	14	6	4	2	1	11	6	7	5	2	25	12
SOUTHPORT	10	3	1	1	6	3	1	2	2	6	11	4	3	3	12	14

OPPONENTS	P	HOME					AWAY					COMBINED				
		W	D	L	F	A	W	D	L	F	A	W	D	L	F	A
STAFFORD RANGERS	28	9	3	2	22	12	3	7	4	17	18	12	10	6	39	30
STALYBRIDGE CELTIC	12	5	0	1	11	9	2	2	2	12	11	7	2	3	23	20
STEVENAGE BOROUGH	8	1	0	3	4	6	0	3	1	3	7	1	3	4	7	13
SUTTON UNITED	10	3	1	1	11	8	2	1	2	7	13	5	2	3	18	21
TELFORD TOWN	38	10	2	7	35	30	7	4	8	23	24	17	6	15	59	54
TROWBRIDGE	6	2	1	0	8	3	2	0	1	4	3	4	1	1	12	6
WEALDSTONE	16	3	0	5	9	12	1	2	5	9	17	4	2	10	18	29
WELLING UNITED	24	4	3	5	20	20	3	3	6	14	19	7	6	11	34	39
WEYMOUTH	20	5	2	3	14	9	2	1	7	9	22	7	3	10	23	31
WITTON ALBION	6	2	1	0	4	2	1	0	2	3	5	3	1	2	7	7
WOKING	12	2	1	3	6	3	1	2	6	3	9	3	3	6	12	12
WORCESTER CITY	12	3	1	2	6	3	3	1	2	13	11	6	2	4	19	14
WYCOMBE WANDERERS	14	4	1	2	11	8	3	2	2	9	9	7	3	4	20	17
YEOVIL TOWN	28	10	3	1	33	13	4	5	5	14	16	14	8	6	47	29

KETTERING TOWN LEAGUE FORM 1979-1998

Season	League	HOME						AWAY					COMBINED						POS	Gates Total	League Aver.
		P	W	D	L	F	A	W	D	L	F	A	W	D	L	F	A	Pts			
1979-80	APL	38	9	5	5	29	26	6	8	5	26	24	15	13	10	55	50	43	7th	36726	1932
1980-81	APL	38	13	4	2	38	12	8	5	6	28	25	21	9	8	66	37	51	2nd	31816	1674
1981-82	APL	42	6	7	8	35	32	3	6	12	29	44	9	13	20	64	76	40	19th	26098	1242
1982-83	APL	42	9	5	7	45	37	2	2	17	24	62	11	7	24	69	99	40	19th	21666	1031
1983-84	APL	42	8	3	10	31	31	4	6	11	22	36	12	9	21	53	67	37	19th	21102	1004
1984-85	GOLA	42	9	6	6	37	22	6	6	9	31	37	15	12	15	68	59	48	12th	24012	1143
1985-86	GOLA	42	11	6	4	37	24	4	9	8	31	29	15	15	12	68	53	49	9th	23304	1109
1986-87	GMVC	42	8	5	8	35	28	4	6	11	19	38	12	11	19	54	66	47	16th	19729	939
1987-88	GMVC	42	13	5	3	37	20	9	4	8	31	28	22	9	11	68	48	75	3rd	28923	1377
1988-89	GMVC	40	16	1	3	35	15	7	6	7	21	24	23	7	10	56	39	76	2nd	50212	2510
1989-90	GMVC	42	13	5	3	35	15	5	7	9	31	38	18	12	12	66	53	66	5th	46362	2207
1990-91	GMVC	42	12	6	3	38	19	11	5	5	29	26	23	11	8	67	45	80	4th	54007	2571
1991-92	GMVC	42	12	6	3	44	23	8	6	7	28	27	20	13	9	72	50	73	3rd	39579	1884
1992-93	GMVC	42	10	5	6	36	28	4	8	9	25	35	14	13	15	61	63	55	13th	30534	1454
1993-94	GMVC	42	9	7	5	23	14	10	8	3	23	10	19	14	8	46	24	72	2nd	42540	2025
1994-95	GMVC	42	12	5	4	40	25	7	9	9	33	31	19	10	13	73	56	67	6th	38584	1837
1995-96	GMVC	42	9	5	7	38	32	4	4	13	30	52	13	9	20	68	84	48	16th	29962	1426
1996-97	GMVC	42	9	4	8	30	28	5	5	11	23	34	14	9	19	53	62	51	14th	35886	1708
1997-98	GMVC	42	8	6	7	29	29	5	7	9	24	31	13	13	16	53	60	52	14th	31343	1492
TOTALS		788	196	96	102	673	460	112	114	168	495	631	308	210	270	1168	1091	1073			

AP LEAMINGTON

Season	V	Comp	F-A	Att:	Poppies Scorers
1979-80	H	APL	1-1	2211	Flannagan
	A	APL	3-1	566	Evans 2, Phipps
	A	ALC2	4-0	773	Hughes, Clayton, Phipps, Phillips
1980-81	H	APL	3-0	1354	Evans, Easthall, Pownall
	A	APL	3-3	569	Evans, Atkins, Phipps
1981-82	H	APL	1-2	1273	Hofbauer
	A	APL	3-3	497	Hofbauer 2, Atkins
1982-83	H	FAC4Q	3-1	1437	Murphy, Banton 2

ALTRINCHAM

Season	V	Comp	F-A	Att:	Poppies Scorers
1979-80	H	APL	1-2	2867	Own goal
	A	APL	0-0	1591	
1980-81	H	APL	1-1	1833	Guy
	A	APL	1-4	2201	Evans
	A	APLCF1	0-2	1887	
	H	APLCF2	2-1	2095	Atkins, Guy
1981-82	H	APL	5-4	1425	Roberts, Atkins 2, Evans, Haverson
	A	APL	1-2	937	Atkins
1982-83	H	APL	3-2	1157	Murphy 2, Banton
	A	APL	1-3	747	Pownall
1983-84	H	APL	1-1	881	Hofbauer
	A	APL	1-1	1130	Denyer
1984-85	H	GOLA	1-2	871	Keast
	A	GOLA	1-2	1085	Jeffrey
	H	BLT3	1-2	1102	Shrieves
1985-86	H	GOLA	2-2	1255	McGowan, Smith
	A	GOLA	2-2	1059	McGowan 2
1986-87	H	GMVC	0-2	1102	
	A	GMVC	1-4	1705	Jeffrey
	A	GMACC3	2-2	602	Smith, Crawley
	H	GMACC3R	2-0	750	Smith, Crawley
1987-88	H	GMVC	1-2	1186	Vinter
	A	GMVC	2-2	1084	Ward, Murphy
	A	FAT2	1-1	881	Richardson
	H	FAT2R	2-3	1021	Keast, Smith
1988-89	H	GMVC	0-1	3201	
	A	GMVC	2-1	1103	Moss, Richardson
1989-90	H	GMVC	3-0	2135	Collins, Cooke 2

	A	GMVC	1-1	554	Cooke
1990-91	H	GMVC	1-1	4145	Cooke
	A	GMVC	2-3	1970	Ritchie, Graham
1991-92	H	GMVC	5-0	1347	Graham 2, North, Hill 2
	A	GMVC	1-1	1293	Christie
1992-93	H	GMVC	1-1	1299	Brown
	A	GMVC	0-3	810	
1993-94	H	GMVC	1-0	1681	Roderick
	A	GMVC	1-1	979	Reed
1994-95	H	GMVC	2-2	1706	Alford 2
	A	GMVC	4-2	702	Brown, Holden, Thomas, Alford
1995-96	H	GMVC	4-2	1369	Alford 3, Scott
	A	GMVC	3-1	969	Alford 2, Stringfellow
1996-97	H	GMVC	3-1	1039	Lyne, Norman 2
	A	GMVC	3-4	791	Gaunt, Pearson 2

AYLESBURY UNITED

Season	V	Comp	F-A	Att:	Poppies Scorers
1986-87	A	GMACCSF	2-0	746	Heywood, Daley
1987-88	A	FAT1	1-1	1222	Smith
	H	FAT1R	5-1	1239	Richardson 2, Murphy 3
1988-89	H	GMVC	5-2	1824	Keast, Moss 2, Cooke 2
	A	GMVC	1-0	1503	Moss 2

BANGOR CITY

Season	V	Comp	F-A	Att:	Poppies Scorers
1979-80	H	APL	0-1	1788	
	A	APL	1-1	920	Clayton
1980-81	H	APL	3-1	1462	Hofbauer, Martin, Guy
	A	APL	1-0	287	Evans
1982-83	H	APL	3-4	1023	Murphy 3
	A	APL	2-4	508	Murphy, Hamill
	A	ALC1/1	1-6	720	Goode
	H	ALC1/2	1-1	556	Murphy
1983-84	H	APL	1-3	923	Dawson
	A	APL	1-3	490	McGoldrick

BARNET

Season	V	Comp	F-A	Att:	Poppies Scorers
1979-80	H	APL	1-0	1899	Hickton
	A	APL	2-0	803	Evans, Hofbauer
1980-81	H	APL	2-1	1360	Curtis 2
	A	APL	1-0	655	Atkins
	H	ALC3	1-1	1331	Atkins
	A	ALC3R	4-1	1337	Evans, Suddards, Atkins, Phipps
1981-82	H	APL	5-2	1157	Murphy 2, Hofbauer, Evans 2
	A	APL	1-2	675	Evans
1982-83	H	APL	3-1	1039	Murphy 2, Goode
	A	APL	3-2	610	Murphy 2, Hamill
1983-84	H	APL	0-1	918	
	A	APL	3-0	610	Hofbauer 2, Kelly
1984-85	H	GOLA	4-0	1216	Thacker, Smith 2, Jenas
	A	GOLA	2-4	774	Alexander 2
1985-86	H	GOLA	1-1	1103	Smith
	A	GOLA	0-3	622	
1986-87	H	GMVC	1-1	1039	Own goal
	A	GMVC	2-1	1735	Kellock, Murphy
1987-88	H	GMVC	1-1	2245	Crawley
	A	GMVC	0-4	2141	
1988-89	H	GMVC	3-1	2534	Fuccillo, Cooke 2
	A	GMVC	2-3	3019	Cooke, Griffith
1989-90	H	GMVC	3-2	2204	Slack, Wright A, Cooke
	A	GMVC	1-4	3480	Lewis
	A	BLT1	2-3	786	Genovese, Graham
1990-91	H	GMVC	1-3	4540	Emson
	A	GMVC	1-0	4261	Hunt

BARROW

Season	V	Comp	F-A	Att:	Poppies Scorers
1979-80	H	APL	0-4	1631	
	A	APL	2-1	796	Clayton, Haverson
1980-81	H	APL	0-1	1565	
	A	APL	1-2	674	Haverson
	A	ALCSF1	2-0	1013	Duggan, Phipps
	H	ALCSF2	5-1	1245	Evans 2, Atkins, Clarke, Phipps
1981-82	H	APL	0-2	1113	
	A	APL	2-7	512	Murphy, Hofbauer
1982-83	H	APL	3-1	889	Duggan 2, Murphy
	A	APL	0-2	684	
1984-85	H	GOLA	0-0	1356	

	A	GOLA	1-0	707	Jeffrey
1985-86	H	GOLA	4-2	984	Keast 2, Fee, Hines
	A	GOLA	0-1	487	
1989-90	H	GMVC	2-0	1170	Wright A, Cooke
	A	GMVC	0-1	1109	
1990-91	H	GMVC	2-0	1350	Bancroft, Cooke
	A	GMVC	1-0	2252	Hunt
	A	FAT2	0-0	3033	
	H	FAT2R	2-1	2522	Slack, Quow
1991-92	H	GMVC	3-2	1750	Graham, Brown, own goal
	A	GMVC	0-0	1384	

BATH CITY

Season	V	Comp	F-A	Att:	Poppies Scorers
1979-80	H	APL	1-2	2164	Evans
	A	APL	0-3	1128	
1980-81	H	APL	2-2	1508	Guy 2
	A	APL	0-0	1030	
1981-82	H	APL	1-3	1623	Murphy
	A	APL	2-3	803	Murphy 2
1982-83	H	APL	4-2	964	Murphy, Poplar, Evans, Collier
	A	APL	1-2	808	Goode
1983-84	H	APL	0-0	746	
	A	APL	1-1	637	Dawson
1984-85	H	GOLA	1-2	1146	Alexander
	A	GOLA	6-1	906	Shrieves 2, Alexander 2, Smith, Jeffrey
1985-86	H	GOLA	2-0	951	Jeffrey, Hines
	A	GOLA	1-1	402	Kabia
1986-87	H	GMVC	2-0	808	Kellock, Genovese
	A	GMVC	2-1	629	Genovese 2
1987-88	H	GMVC	1-1	841	Smith
	A	GMVC	0-2	613	
1990-91	H	GMVC	1-1	1570	Cooke
	A	GMVC	3-3	1069	Cooke 2, Graham
1991-92	H	GMVC	2-2	2379	Keast, Christie
	A	GMVC	1-1	699	Own goal
1992-93	H	GMVC	0-1	1185	
	A	GMVC	0-0	386	
1993-94	H	GMVC	0-1	2044	
	A	GMVC	3-0	864	Brown, Martin, Roderick
1994-95	H	GMVC	0-0	1218	
	A	GMVC	0-2	689	
1995-96	H	GMVC	3-0	1767	Alford, Pope, Stringfellow
	A	GMVC	1-3	612	Parsons

| 1996-97 | H | GMVC | 1-0 | 1444 | Norman |
| | A | GMVC | 2-0 | 660 | Pope, Mustafa |

BOSTON UNITED

Season	V	Comp	F-A	Att:	Poppies Scorers
1979-80	H	APL	3-1	1854	Clayton 2, Evans
	A	APL	0-1	2127	
1980-81	H	APL	0-0	2608	
	A	APL	1-2	1755	Atkins
1981-82	H	APL	1-1	1506	Atkins
	A	APL	2-4	1456	Murphy, Phipps
	A	FAC1	1-0	2826	Atkins
1982-83	H	APL	2-0	1118	Murphy, Duggan
	A	APL	1-2	1562	Goode
1983-84	H	APL	2-1	1324	Masson,Bradd
	A	APL	1-3	1179	Denyer
1984-85	H	GOLA	2-1	1179	Smith 2
	A	GOLA	1-3	1402	Own goal
	A	BLT1/1	4-0	1004	Keast, Fee, Dawson 2
	H	BLT1/2	3-2	902	Jeffrey, Jenas, Sellers
1985-86	H	GOLA	3-1	1951	Crawley 3
	A	GOLA	1-4	1553	Crawley
1986-87	H	GMVC	1-2	848	Smith
	A	GMVC	1-2	981	Smith
	H	GMACC2	3-2	902	Keast, Jeffrey 2
1987-88	H	GMVC	3-0	840	Kellock, Keast, Smith
	A	GMVC	2-0	1815	Smith, Richardson
1988-89	H	GMVC	1-2	3231	Griffith
	A	GMVC	1-1	3343	Moss
1989-90	H	GMVC	5-0	3951	Moss 2, Cooke 2, Beech
	A	GMVC	2-1	2630	Moss, Cooke
1990-91	H	GMVC	1-1	3207	Slack
	A	GMVC	2-1	3331	Bancroft, Moss
1991-92	H	GMVC	1-3	3207	Slack
	A	GMVC	1-1	2919	Nicol
1992-93	H	GMVC	3-3	2592	Brown 2, Martin
	A	GMVC	1-0	1481	Brown

BROMSGROVE ROVERS

Season	V	Comp	F-A	Att:	Poppies Scorers
1992-93	H	GMVC	3-2	1328	Brown 2, Murphy
	A	GMVC	1-1	1297	Brown
	H	FAT1	0-0	1723	
	A	FAT1R	1-4	1269	Riley
1993-94	H	GMVC	0-1	2620	
	A	GMVC	4-0	1253	Graham 2, Dempsey, Costello
1994-95	H	GMVC	0-1	2009	
	A	GMVC	4-2	938	Alford 3, Brown
	A	BLTF1	1-4	1393	Clarke
	H	BLTF2	1-6	1311	Alford
1995-96	H	GMVC	2-2	2006	Oxbrow, Alford
	A	GMVC	2-3	824	Benjamin, Dowling
	H	FAC4Q	0-0	2427	
	A	FAC4QR	2-2	1426	Scott, Alford
	H	FAC4Q2R	1-2	2283	Alford
	A	SCCSF1	0-2	650	
	H	SCCSF2	2-1	773	Gynn, Mustafa
1996-97	H	GMVC	2-0	1578	Lynch, Mustafa
	A	GMVC	2-1	898	Nugent, Mustafa

CHELTENHAM TOWN

Season	V	Comp	F-A	Att:	Poppies Scorers
1985-86	H	GOLA	2-1	532	Keast, Jeffrey
	A	GOLA	1-5	1221	Smith
	H	BLT1/1	0-1	920	
	A	BLT1/2	1-5	1293	Crawley
1986-87	H	GMVC	0-0	850	
	A	GMVC	1-3	1259	Kellock
1987-88	H	GMVC	1-1	1149	Keast
	A	GMVC	2-1	1122	Murphy, Smith
1988-89	H	GMVC	2-0	2165	Creane, Moss
	A	GMVC	1-2	2241	Cooke
1989-90	H	GMVC	1-0	2340	Genovese
	A	GMVC	1-1	1258	Jones
1990-91	H	GMVC	5-1	1761	Bancroft, Brown 2, Jones, own goal
	A	GMVC	2-2	1437	Goodwin, Cooke
1991-92	H	GMVC	3-0	1336	Huxford, North 2
	A	GMVC	3-0	1006	Brown, Graham, Hill
1997-98	H	GMVC	0-1	1274	
	A	GMVC	0-2	1219	

CHORLEY

Season	V	Comp	F-A	Att:	Poppies Scorers
1988-89	H	GMVC	3-0	2578	Fuccillo, Cooke, Griffith
	A	GMVC	1-0	1325	Edwards
1989-90	H	GMVC	2-1	1152	Moss, Cooke
	A	GMVC	2-2	608	Cooke 2

COLCHESTER UNITED

Season	V	Comp	F-A	Att:	Poppies Scorers
1990-91	H	GMVC	1-0	5020	Keast
	A	GMVC	1-3	5048	Brown
1991-92	H	GMVC	2-2	4100	Hill 2
	A	GMVC	1-3	6303	North
	A	BLT1	0-4	1298	

DAGENHAM

Season	V	Comp	F-A	Att:	Poppies Scorers
1981-82	H	APL	3-1	946	Hofbauer, Murphy, Haverson
	A	APL	1-2	1217	Murphy
1982-83	H	APL	1-2	932	Wright
	A	APL	3-2	740	Murphy, Evans, Chamberlain
1983-84	H	APL	2-2	1243	Hofbauer, Needham
	A	APL	0-2	490	
1984-85	H	GOLA	0-1	1246	
	A	GOLA	1-2	560	Jeffrey
1985-86	H	GOLA	0-2	896	
	A	GOLA	0-1	536	
1986-87	H	GMVC	3-1	765	Kellock, own goal, Jeffrey
	A	GMVC	2-1	499	Smith, Kellock
1987-88	H	GMVC	3-0	810	Keast 2, Crawley
	A	GMVC	5-0	469	Tillson, Murphy, Richardson, Smith 2

DAGENHAM & REDBRIDGE

Season	V	Comp	F-A	Att:	Poppies Scorers
1992-93	H	GMVC	0-0	1321	
	A	GMVC	2-1	1255	Donovan 2

1993-94	H	GMVC	1-1	2161	Brown
	A	GMVC	3-2	1376	Brown 2, Graham
1994-95	H	GMVC	2-2	1581	Alford, Thomas
	A	GMVC	1-2	1002	Arnold
	H	BLTS/F1	0-2	1033	
	A	BLTS/F2	4-2	750	Arnold 2, Brown, Thomas
1995-96	H	GMVC	2-0	1616	Alford, Stringfellow
	A	GMVC	2-1	730	Own Goal, Thomas

DARLINGTON

Season	V	Comp	F-A	Att:	Poppies Scorers
1989-90	H	GMVC	1-3	3721	Keast
	A	GMVC	1-2	3880	Cooke

DARTFORD

Season	V	Comp	F-A	Att:	Poppies Scorers
1981-82	H	APL	4-4	1154	Atkins 2, Hofbauer, Shelton
	A	APL	2-2	604	Evans 2
1984-85	H	GOLA	0-2	858	
	A	GOLA	1-0	913	Muir
1985-86	H	GOLA	2-2	1016	Jeffrey 2
	A	GOLA	2-0	456	Kabia, Jeffrey
1988-89	H	FAC1	2-1	3024	Lewis, Griffith

DOVER ATHLETIC

Season	V	Comp	F-A	Att:	Poppies Scorers
1993-94	H	GMVC	1-0	2134	Ashby N
	A	GMVC	1-0	974	Taylor
1994-95	H	GMVC	1-0	1575	Graham
	A	GMVC	2-0	1057	Alford, Arnold
1995-96	H	GMVC	2-2	1332	Pope, Haworth
	A	GMVC	1-2	1045	Alford
	H	GMVC	1-1	1290	Nyamah
	A	GMVC	1-0	966	Slawson
1997-98	H	GMVC	2-1	1056	Tucker, Norman
	A	GMVC	0-0	781	
	A	SCC1	3-1	520	Wilkes, Costello, Norman

ENFIELD

Season	V	Comp	F-A	Att:	Poppies Scorers
1981-82	H	APL	0-1	1311	
	A	APL	1-1	730	Atkins
1982-83	H	APL	0-2	1598	
	A	APL	2-5	1025	Murphy 2
1983-84	H	APL	1-0	1333	Own goal
	A	APL	2-2	683	Murphy, Banton
1984-85	H	GOLA	4-3	1386	Smith 3, Shrieves
	A	GOLA	3-5	758	Jeffrey 2, Smith
1985-86	H	GOLA	2-1	1354	Jeffrey, Shrieves
	A	GOLA	1-1	570	Keast
1986-87	H	GMVC	2-0	1005	Smith 2
	A	GMVC	0-0	1035	
1987-88	H	GMVC	2-1	1070	Murphy, Smith
	A	GMVC	0-2	884	
1988-89	H	GMVC	0-1	2671	
	A	GMVC	1-1	856	Cooke
1989-90	H	GMVC	3-2	2054	Edwards, Cooke 2
	A	GMVC	3-0	851	Moss, Cooke 2

FARNBOROUGH TOWN

Season	V	Comp	F-A	Att:	Poppies Scorers
1989-90	H	GMVC	1-1	2706	Richardson
	A	GMVC	1-1	934	Richardson
1991-92	H	GMVC	1-2	1993	Bancroft
	A	GMVC	3-1	1086	Graham, Hill, Brown
1992-93	H	GMVC	2-1	1395	Tomlinson, Nuttell
	A	GMVC	2-3	1007	Bancroft, Brown
1994-95	H	GMVC	4-1	1578	Arnold, own goal, Stringfellow, Graham
	A	GMVC	0-0	666	
1995-96	H	GMVC	0-2	1260	
	A	GMVC	1-1	1037	Scott
1996-97	H	GMVC	3-1	1092	Berry, Venables, Lynch
	A	GMVC	2-0	1106	May 2
	H	SCC2	0-2	503	
1997-98	H	GMVC	2-1	1433	Mutchell, Norman
	A	GMVC	2-3	771	Nuttell, Norman

FISHER ATHLETIC

Season	V	Comp	F-A	Att:	Poppies Scorers
1987-88	H	GMVC	2-1	1135	Lewis, Kellock
	A	GMVC	1-1	471	Smith
1988-89	H	GMVC	2-1	2739	Moss, Cooke
	A	GMVC	0-3	354	
1989-90	H	GMVC	3-0	2050	Cooke 3
	A	GMVC	1-3	350	Cooke
1990-91	H	GMVC	3-2	2276	Bancroft 3
	A	GMVC	0-0	653	

FRICKLEY ATHLETIC

Season	V	Comp	F-A	Att:	Poppies Scorers
1980-81	H	APL	6-1	1352	Hofbauer 3, Easthall, Evans, Martin
	A	APL	1-1	706	Own goal
1981-82	H	APL	0-0	1475	
	A	APL	2-3	535	Atkins 2
1982-83	H	APL	4-1	1027	Banton 2, Murphy, Evans
	A	APL	2-3	401	Wright 2
1983-84	H	APL	0-1	668	
	A	APL	1-1	412	Dawson
1984-85	H	GOLA	5-0	760	Jeffrey 2, Jenas, Bolton, Alexander
	A	GOLA	0-3	310	
1985-86	H	GOLA	2-0	768	Smith, Fee
	A	GOLA	0-3	576	
1986-87	H	GMVC	1-2	810	Jeffrey
	A	GMVC	2-2	498	Crawley, Richardson

GATESHEAD

Season	V	Comp	F-A	Att:	Poppies Scorers
1983-84	H	APL	3-0	894	Keast, Murphy 2
	A	APL	2-1	312	Murphy, McGowan
1984-85	H	GOLA	1-1	985	Own goal
	A	GOLA	4-1	219	Thrower, Wharton, Shrieves, Smith

164

1986-87	H	GMVC	5-1	815	Tillson, Crawley 2, Kellock, Keast
	A	GMVC	1-1	354	Keast
1990-91	H	GMVC	1-0	1831	Jones
	A	GMVC	2-1	914	Brown, Hunt
1991-92	H	GMVC	1-1	1497	North
	A	GMVC	0-0	420	
1992-93	H	GMVC	2-0	1455	Riley, Wood
	A	GMVC	1-1	478	Harris
1993-94	H	GMVC	0-0	1783	
	A	GMVC	0-0	553	
1994-95	H	GMVC	2-4	1776	Alford, Graham
	A	GMVC	0-0	538	
1995-96	H	GMVC	1-0	1179	Alford
	A	GMVC	1-1	712	Alford
1996-97	H	GMVC	4-1	1329	Lynch 3, Norman
	A	GMVC	1-1	767	Norman
1997-98	H	GMVC	3-0	1201	Pearson 2, Adams
	A	GMVC	0-2	468	

GRAVESEND & NORTHFLEET

Season	V	Comp	F-A	Att:	Poppies Scorers
1979-80	H	APL	0-0	1308	
	A	APL	2-2	1079	Clayton 2
1980-81	H	APL	2-0	1755	Evans, Hofbauer
	A	APL	0-1	1094	
	A	FAT1	3-2	1024	Evans 2, own goal
1981-82	H	APL	2-1	1157	Atkins, Duggan
	A	APL	3-1	932	Murphy 2, Hofbauer
1988-89	A	FAT2	1-1	1119	Beech
	H	FAT2R	1-2	2801	Moss

HALIFAX TOWN

Season	V	Comp	F-A	Att:	Poppies Scorers
1988-89	H	FAC3*	1-1	5800	Griffiths
	A	FAC3R*	3-2	5632	Lewis, Cooke 2
1993-94	H	GMVC	0-1	2409	
	A	GMVC	0-0	1810	
1994-95	H	GMVC	5-1	1330	Arnold 3, Thomas, Brown
	A	GMVC	1-2	1021	Alford
1995-96	H	GMVC	1-2	1317	Benjamin

	A	GMVC	0-2	929	
1996-97	H	GMVC	4-1	1541	Mustafa, Nugent, Pope, Lynch
	A	GMVC	1-2	790	Norman
1997-98	H	GMVC	1-1	2276	Van Dulleman
	A	GMVC	0-3	1836	

*Halifax were a Football League Club, not in the Conference.

HAYES

Season	V	Comp	F-A	Att:	Poppies Scorers
1996-97	H	GMVC	2-2	1608	Nyamah, Stock
	A	GMVC	1-2	468	Harmon
1997-98	H	GMVC	1-1	1006	Vowden
	A	GMVC	1-0	506	Pearson

HEDNESFORD TOWN

Season	V	Comp	F-A	Att:	Poppies Scorers
1995-96	H	GMVC	2-0	1712	Haworth, Alford
	A	GMVC*	1-2	1584	Haworth
	A	GMVC	0-1	1049	
1996-97	H	GMVC	0-2	766	
	A	GMVC	0-0	1121	
1997-98	H	GMVC	2-1	2051	Sandeman, Vowden
	A	GMVC	1-1	1911	Berry

*Abandoned after 51 minutes due to floodlight failure.

HEREFORD UNITED

Season	V	Comp	F-A	Att:	Poppies Scorers
1997-98	H	GMVC	1-2	1404	Costello
	A	GMVC	2-3	2130	Norman, Pearson

166

KIDDERMINSTER HARRIERS

Season	V	Comp	F-A	Att:	Poppies Scorers
1983-84	H	APL	4-2	1010	Kelly, McGoldrick, Hofbauer, Murphy
	A	APL	1-3	591	Murphy
1984-85	H	GOLA	2-2	751	Thacker, Jeffrey
	A	GOLA	2-2	558	Keast, Jenas
1985-86	H	GOLA	2-2	1015	Crawley, Fee
	A	GOLA	0-0	579	
1986-87	H	GMVC	0-2	830	
	A	GMVC	1-2	1231	Richardson
1987-88	H	GMVC	1-1	1223	Smith
	A	GMVC	1-2	1521	Smith
1988-89	H	GMVC	2-1	4377	Griffith, Gallagher
	A	GMVC	1-1	1551	Wright A
1989-90	H	GMVC	0-2	2725	
	A	GMVC	3-2	1335	Cooke 2, Wright A
1990-91	H	GMVC	4-1	3112	Slack, Moss, Cooke 2
	A	GMVC	0-3	1517	
1991-92	H	GMVC	2-1	1532	Brown, Graham
	A	GMVC	3-2	1243	Graham 2, Gavin
1992-93	H	GMVC	1-2	1365	Brown
	A	GMVC	0-0	1608	
	A	BLT1	0-3	624	
1993-94	H	GMVC	1-1	2927	Costello
	A	GMVC	2-0	1274	Taylor, Loughlan
	A	FAC1	0-3	3775	
1994-95	H	GMVC	0-0	3049	
	A	GMVC	3-1	1417	Clarke, Arnold, Graham
	A	BLT2	5-1	914	Brown 2, Stringfellow, Magee, Martin
1995-96	H	GMVC	2-0	1376	Harmon, Mustafa
	A	GMVC	0-1	1949	
1996-97	H	GMVC	3-1	2305	Lyne, Norman, Lynch
	A	GMVC	0-4	2754	
1997-98	H	GMVC	2-2	1576	Pearson, Wilkes
	A	GMVC	1-4	1874	Wilkes

LEEK TOWN

Season	V	Comp	F-A	Att:	Poppies Scorers
1997-98	H	GMVC	1-0	1287	Adams
	A	GMVC	4-0	662	Sandeman, Costello, Wilkes 2

167

LINCOLN CITY

Season	V	Comp	F-A	Att:	Poppies Scorers
1987-88	H	GMVC	2-0	4135	Richardson, own goal
	A	GMVC	1-0	3145	Crawley

MACCLESFIELD TOWN

Season	V	Comp	F-A	Att:	Poppies Scorers
1984-85	A	FAT3Q	2-0	664	Alexander, Smith
1987-88	H	GMVC	3-2	1319	Lewis, Keast, Murphy
	A	GMVC	0-0	1502	
1988-89	H	GMVC	1-0	3253	Fuccillo
	A	GMVC	1-0	2196	Moss
1989-90	H	GMVC	0-0	1550	
	A	GMVC	1-3	1598	Slack
1990-91	H	GMVC	2-0	1814	Goodwin, Bancroft
	A	GMVC	2-1	1154	Goodwin, Walwyn
1991-92	H	GMVC	2-0	1367	Brown 2
	A	GMVC	2-0	940	Brown, Christie
1992-93	H	GMVC	1-0	1209	Hill
	A	GMVC	0-1	731	
1993-94	H	GMVC	0-1	2158	
	A	GMVC	0-0	933	
1994-95	H	GMVC	1-0	2130	Alford
	A	GMVC	0-1	947	
1995-96	H	GMVC	2-2	1433	Nyamah 2
	A	GMVC	1-1	1320	Stringfellow
1996-97	H	GMVC	1-4	3451	Lyne
	A	GMVC	0-2	1250	

MAIDSTONE UNITED

Season	V	Comp	F-A	Att:	Poppies Scorers
1979-80	H	APL	1-1	1507	Evans
	A	APL	3-1	1004	Phipps, Clayton, Ashby
1980-81	H	APL	3-0	2300	Evans, Phipps, Atkins
	A	APL	2-1	774	Evans 2
	H	FAC1	1-1	2880	Guy
	A	FAC1R	0-0	3156	
	A	FAC1R2	1-3	3098	Middleton
1981-82	H	APL	2-2	1531	Evans 2

	V	Comp	F-A	Att:	Poppies Scorers
	A	APL	0-2	780	
1982-83	H	APL	1-3	1090	Banton
	A	APL	1-5	1335	Banton
1983-84	H	APL	0-2	954	
	A	APL	0-1	1036	
1984-85	H	GOLA	2-0	626	Wharton, Alexander
	A	GOLA	0-3	930	
1985-86	H	GOLA	2-0	1459	Keast 2
	A	GOLA	0-0	753	
1986-87	H	GMVC	1-2	1050	Jeffrey
	A	GMVC	0-3	804	
1987-88	H	GMVC	0-2	887	
	A	GMVC	3-2	825	Murphy 2, Curtis
1988-89	H	GMVC	3-3	2010	Moss 2, Fuccillo
	A	GMVC	0-0	2861	
1991-92	A	FAC2	2-1	2750	Brown P, own goal

MERTHYR TYDFILL

Season	V	Comp	F-A	Att:	Poppies Scorers
1979-80	A	FAT1	0-3	1756	
1989-90	H	GMVC	2-0	2215	Richardson, Cooke
	A	GMVC	2-3	2300	Moss, Griffith
1990-91	H	GMVC	2-0	2589	Huxford, Bancroft
	A	GMVC	3-1	851	Goodwin, Graham 2
1991-92	H	GMVC	3-1	1616	Nicol, Hill 2
	A	GMVC	1-4	570	Hill
1992-93	H	GMVC	1-3	1354	Riley
	A	GMVC	1-2	486	Price
1993-94	H	GMVC	0-0	1702	
	A	GMVC	1-0	527	Dempsey
1994-95	H	GMVC	4-1	1546	Alford, Brown 2, Thomas
	A	GMVC	1-2	702	Alford

MORECAMBE

Season	V	Comp	F-A	Att:	Poppies Scorers
1995-96	H	GMVC	2-3	1124	Oxbrow, Benjamin
	A	GMVC	3-5	1098	Stott, Alford, Scott
1996-97	H	GMVC	0-2	1362	
	A	GMVC	2-5	1205	Gaunt, Stock
1997-98	H	GMVC	1-1	1156	Pearson
	A	GMVC	3-1	1241	Pearson, Adams 2

NEWPORT COUNTY

Season	V	Comp	F-A	Att:	Poppies Scorers
1988-89	A	GMVC	2-1	1871	Griffith 2

Newport County went out of business and dropped out of the GMVC.The Poppies lost the three points gained and their promotion hopes were given a severe jolt.

NORTHWICH VICTORIA

Season	V	Comp	F-A	Att:	Poppies Scorers
1979-80	H	APL	1-0	1872	Phillips
	A	APL	2-2	1620	Ashby R, Phipps
	H	ALCSF1	0-0	1643	
	A	ALCSF2	1-3	1395	Evans
1980-81	H	APL	3-3	1818	Evans 2, Martin
	A	APL	1-1	1469	Evans
1981-82	H	APL	0-0	1306	
	A	APL	0-2	737	
	A	ALC2/1	3-3	758	Atkins, Murphy, Evans
	H	ALC2/2	0-2	1276	
1982-83	H	APL	1-4	1004	Murphy
	A	APL	1-2	943	Hofbauer
1983-84	H	APL	1-0	913	Hofbauer
	A	APL	0-4	1194	
1984-85	H	GOLA	2-2	1126	Jeffrey 2
	A	GOLA	2-1	769	Shrieves, Alexander
	H	BLT2	1-0	657	Shrieves
1985-86	H	GOLA	2-1	1367	McGowan, Watson
	A	GOLA	0-0	519	
1986-87	H	GMVC	1-0	942	Crawley
	A	GMVC	0-0	768	
1987-88	H	GMVC	3-1	1035	Ward, Smith, Crawley
	A	GMVC	1-0	793	Smith
	H	GMACC3	2-3	661	Ward, Murphy
1988-89	H	GMVC	2-1	1083	Griffith, Lawrence
	A	GMVC	1-1	861	Edwards
1989-90	H	GMVC	3-1	1605	Beech, Cooke, Jones
	A	GMVC	2-2	709	Slack, Moss
1990-91	H	GMVC	1-0	2452	Keast
	A	GMVC	1-0	931	Graham
1991-92	H	GMVC	1-0	1513	Bancroft

170

Season	V	Comp	F-A	Att:	Poppies Scorers
	A	GMVC	3-4	665	Graham, Bancroft, Hill
1992-93	H	GMVC	2-1	1221	Riley 2
	A	GMVC	2-2	721	Docker, Bancroft
1993-94	H	GMVC	0-0	1767	
	A	GMVC	1-1	783	Whitehouse
1994-95	H	GMVC	3-3	1874	Taylor, Thomas, Alford
	A	GMVC	2-3	880	Stringfellow, Holden
1995-96	H	GMVC	2-2	912	Alford 2
	A	GMVC	2-6	632	Pope 2
1996-97	H	GMVC	1-0	1378	Wilkes
	A	GMVC	1-2	1055	Pearson
1997-98	H	GMVC	1-3	1156	Sandeman
	A	GMVC	0-0	1131	
	A	FAT2	0-4	1225	

NUNEATON BOROUGH

Season	V	Comp	F-A	Att:	Poppies Scorers
1979-80	H	APL	1-1	1093	Flannagan
	A	APL	2-2	1970	Evans, Phipps
1980-81	H	APL	3-0	1583	Evans, Curtis, Phipps
	A	APL	5-1	1210	Evans 4, Clarke
1982-83	H	APL	0-0	1164	
	A	APL	0-0	1037	
1983-84	H	APL	3-4	1234	Hofbauer 2, Beavon
	A	APL	0-1	921	
1983-84	H	BLT1/1	4-2	1068	Murphy 2, Bradd, Hofbauer
	A	BLT1/2	1-1	885	Hofbauer
1984-85	H	GOLA	1-1	2175	Jeffrey
	A	GOLA	1-1	1330	Fee
1985-86	H	GOLA	1-4	733	Crawley
	A	GOLA	3-0	1016	Kabia, Watson, Crawley
1986-87	H	GMVC	2-2	980	Genovese, Fee
	A	GMVC	0-0	716	

REDBRIDGE FOREST

Season	V	Comp	F-A	Att:	Poppies Scorers
1991-92	H	GMVC	3-2	1304	North, Brown, Graham
	A	GMVC	0-4	726	

REDDITCH UNITED

Season	V	Comp	F-A	Att:	Poppies Scorers
1979-80	H	APL	2-1	1940	Evans, Phipps
	A	APL	1-0	316	Flannagan

RUNCORN

Season	V	Comp	F-A	Att:	Poppies Scorers
1981-82	H	APL	0-0	1390	
	A	APL	2-3	804	Murphy, Hofbauer
1982-83	H	APL	3-1	1041	Goode, Murphy, Palmer
	A	APL	0-6	720	
1983-84	H	APL	1-0	950	Keast
	A	APL	1-4	695	Murphy
	A	BLT2/1	0-4	656	
	H	BLT2/2	1-1	545	Shelton
1984-85	H	GOLA	3-0	957	Keast, Jenas 2
	A	GOLA	2-2	413	Jeffrey, Keast
1985-86	H	GOLA	0-0	583	
	A	GOLA	1-0	565	Smith
	A	FATSF1	0-0	2023	
	H	FATSF2	0-2	4032	
1986-87	H	GMVC	1-1	1015	Smith
	A	GMVC	0-1	604	
	A	GMACC4	2-1	617	Cavener, Smith
1987-88	H	GMVC	0-3	2520	
	A	GMVC	0-1	686	
1988-89	H	GMVC	2-0	2337	Cooke, Moss
	A	GMVC	1-2	766	Griffith
1989-90	H	GMVC	1-1	2239	Moss
	A	GMVC	1-3	1028	Graham
1990-91	H	GMVC	3-0	2238	Nicol, Graham, Hunt
	A	GMVC	1-2	903	Cooke
1991-92	H	GMVC	3-0	1519	Brown, Hill 2
	A	GMVC	0-0	637	
1992-93	H	GMVC	3-3	911	Hodges, Hope, Brown
	A	GMVC	2-2	492	Riley, Murphy
1993-94	H	GMVC	2-2	1476	Brown, Martin
	A	GMVC	0-0	464*	
1994-95	H	GMVC	3-0	2650	Alford 2, Brown
	A	GMVC	2-1	491+	Taylor, Brown
1995-96	H	GMVC	4-0	1583	Stott, Alford, Stringfellow 2
	A	GMVC	2-4	569	Hunter 2

*Played at Northwich Victoria.   + Played at Witton Albion.

RUSHDEN & DIAMONDS

Season	V	Comp	F-A	Att:	Poppies Scorers
1992-93	H	NSCF	2-1	873	Brown, Hodges
1993-94	A	NSCSF	2-3	2353	Dempsey 2
1994-95	A	NSCF	0-1A	2350	(Floodlight failure at half-time)
	A	NSCF*	2-2	1927	Scott, Arnold
	H	NSCFR*	2-2	1509+	Thomas, Stringfellow
1996-97	H	GMVC	1-5	4628	Pearson
	A	GMVC	0-1	5170	
	H	NSCQF	2-1	1837	Norman, May
1997-98	H	GMVC	0-4	4016	
	A	GMVC	0-1	3386	

*Played at the beginning of the 1995-96 season.
+Kettering won 3-1 on penalties.
A Abandoned

SCARBOROUGH

Season	V	Comp	F-A	Att:	Poppies Scorers
1979-80	H	APL	1-0	1758	Jones
	A	APL	0-2	3120	
1980-81	H	APL	1-0	1258	Duggan
	A	APL	2-1	2225	Atkins 2
1981-82	H	APL	1-2	1092	Hofbauer
	A	APL	0-1	1623	
1982-83	H	APL	2-2	1088	Duggan, Hofbauer
	A	APL	0-3	1200	
1983-84	H	APL	2-3	1320	Bradd, Bartlett
	A	APL	0-0	1111	
1984-85	H	GOLA	0-1	1084	
	A	GOLA	0-0	843	
1985-86	H	GOLA	0-0	1348	
	A	GOLA	3-2	520	Crawley 2, Kabia
1986-87	H	GMVC	1-2	1137	Smith
	A	GMVC	0-1	867	

SLOUGH TOWN

Season	V	Comp	F-A	Att:	Poppies Scorers
1985-86	A	FAT2	2-1	871	Fee, Smith
1990-91	H	GMVC	0-0	3002	

	A	GMVC	3-0	1710	Brown, Graham 2
1991-92	H	GMVC	2-3	1830	Graham, Christie
	A	GMVC	2-0	698	Graham 2
1992-93	H	GMVC	5-0	1205	Own goal, Riley 2, Hill 2
	A	GMVC	0-3	1095	
1993-94	H	GMVC	2-0	1434	Costello 2
	A	GMVC	2-0	1122	Taylor, Brown
1995-96	H	GMVC	2-0	1902	Scott, Alford
	A	GMVC	2-1	766	Nyamah, Alford
	A	FAT2	2-1	1058	Scott, Gynn
	H	SCCQF	2-0	646	Pope, Harmon
1996-97	H	GMVC	0-0	1379	
	A	GMVC	1-1	1032	Woodsford
	H	SCC2	1-0	702	May
1997-98	H	GMVC	3-3	1349	Costello, Norman 2
	A	GMVC	1-1	515	Mutchell

SOUTHPORT

Season	V	Comp	F-A	Att:	Poppies Scorers
1993-94	H	GMVC	2-0	1980	Taylor, Thorpe
	A	GMVC	1-0	1026	Whitehouse
1994-95	H	GMVC	1-0	2005	Alford
	A	GMVC	1-1	919	Arnold
1995-96	H	GMVC	1-1	1944	Pope
	A	GMVC	1-6	916	Norman
1996-97	H	GMVC	0-1	1575	
	A	GMVC	2-2	676	Wilkes, Mustafa
1997-98	H	GMVC	3-1	1157	Pearson, Wilkes
	A	GMVC	1-2	973	Pearson

STAFFORD RANGERS

Season	V	Comp	F-A	Att:	Poppies Scorers
1979-80	H	APL	3-6	2656	Jones, Evans, Ashby
	A	APL	0-0	2104	
1980-81	H	APL	1-0	1662	Evans
	A	APL	1-3	1599	Hofbauer
1981-82	H	APL	3-0	855	Duggan, Phipps, Evans
	A	APL	1-1	712	Hofbauer
1982-83	H	APL	2-2	900	Murphy 2
	A	APL	1-1	804	Evans
1985-86	H	GOLA	0-1	1207	
	A	GOLA	0-0	851	

1986-87	H	GMVC	2-2	900	Wood 2
	A	GMVC	2-2	1259	Keast, Kellock
1987-88	H	GMVC	1-0	1060	Lewis
	A	GMVC	1-2	1383	Smith
	A	GMACC	1-0	1185	Murphy
1988-89	H	GMVC	1-0	1836	Moss
	A	GMVC	1-2	1602	Nightingale
1989-90	H	GMVC	0-0	2759	
	A	GMVC	1-1	1201	Lewis
1990-91	H	GMVC	2-0	3272	Keast, Hunt
	A	GMVC	0-0	1551	
1991-92	H	GMVC	2-1	1398	Graham, Hill
	A	GMVC	2-1	1089	Brown, Christie
	H	FAC4Q	0-0	1785	
	A	FAC4QR	2-0	1070	Christie, Jones
1992-93	H	GMVC	2-0	1260	Murphy 2
	A	GMVC	4-2	815	Hope, Brown, Riley, Martin
1993-94	H	GMVC	2-0	1701	Brown, Taylor
	A	GMVC	0-1	1456	
1994-95	H	GMVC	1-0	2018	Alford
	A	GMVC	3-2	774	Stringfellow, Brown, Alford

STALYBRIDGE CELTIC

Season	V	Comp	F-A	Att:	Poppies Scorers
1992-93	H	GMVC	2-0	1130	Donald, Harris
	A	GMVC	0-0	805	
1993-94	H	GMVC	3-2	1949	Oxbrow, Clarke, Martin
	A	GMVC	1-1	630	Price
1994-95	H	GMVC	1-0	1471	Howe
	A	GMVC	4-1	722	Stringfellow 2, Brown, Holden
1995-96	H	GMVC	1-6	962	Dowling
	A	GMVC	2-3	627	Scott, Stott
1996-97	H	GMVC	1-0	1509	Norman
	A	GMVC	1-3	684	Berry
1997-98	H	GMVC	3-1	1547	Vowden, Adams, Costello
	A	GMVC	4-3	564	Pearson, Wilkes, Norman, Costello

STEVENAGE BOROUGH

Season	V	Comp	F-A	Att:	Poppies Scorers
1993-94	H	FAT1	2-1	2414	Wright, Reed
1994-95	H	GMVC	0-2	2532	
	A	GMVC	2-2	1808	Arnold, Alford
1995-96	H	GMVC	1-2	1414	Mustafa
	A	GMVC	1-5	2033	Oxbrow
	H	SCC2	2-1	808	Stringfellow, Harmon
	A	FAT3	0-3	2219	
1996-97	H	GMVC	1-2	1874	Norman
	A	GMVC	0-0	2864	
1997-98	H	GMVC	2-0	1488	Wilkes, Pearson
	A	GMVC	0-0	3486	

SUTTON UNITED

Season	V	Comp	F-A	Att:	Poppies Scorers
1985-86	H	FAT1	1-0	773	Shrieves
1986-87	H	GMVC	1-4	1133	Smith
	A	GMVC	0-8	525	
1987-88	H	GMVC	2-2	1853	Crawley, Edwards
	A	GMVC	2-2	655	Murphy 2
1988-89	H	GMVC	1-0	1361	Moss
	A	GMVC	2-0	1438	Gallagher, Cooke
1989-90	H	GMVC	2-0	1176	Wright, Jones
	A	GMVC	1-2	1104	Slack
1990-91	H	GMVC	5-2	843	Graham 3, Jones 2
	A	GMVC	2-1	1184	Keast, Goodwin
	H	BLTSF1	0-2	1104	
	A	BLTSF2	1-4	707	Graham

TELFORD UNITED

Season	V	Comp	F-A	Att:	Poppies Scorers
1979-80	H	APL	3-2	1508	Clayton, Evans, Flannagan
	A	APL	0-1	718	
1980-81	H	APL	2-1	1249	Atkins, Duggan
	A	APL	2-0	813	Atkins, Hofbauer
1981-82	H	APL	1-3	1142	Murphy

	A	APL	0-1	1151	
1982-83	H	APL	1-2	906	Collier
	A	APL	1-2	1108	Murphy
1983-84	H	APL	4-1	907	Hofbauer, Kelly, Murphy 2
	A	APL	0-1	1336	
1984-85	H	GOLA	4-2	1067	Thacker, Jeffrey, Keast, Alexander
	A	GOLA	1-1	1052	Shrieves
1985-86	H	GOLA	4-0	1074	Dawson, Kabia, Smith, Jeffrey
	A	GOLA	2-2	1147	Keast, Wharton
1986-87	H	GMVC	3-1	814	Lewis, Murphy 2
	A	GMVC	0-2	1057	
	H	GMACC1	0-0	728	
	A	GMACC1R	2-0	851	Lewis, Keast
1987-88	H	GMVC	1-0	1050	Murphy
	A	GMVC	3-2	1208	Keast, Lewis, Daley
1988-89	H	GMVC	1-0	2745	Keast
	A	GMVC	1-0	1023	Griffith
1989-90	H	GMVC	1-1	1957	Cooke
	A	GMVC	3-1	1414	Cooke, Griffith 2
1990-91	H	GMVC	2-5	2068	Bancroft, Graham
	A	GMVC	1-0	1538	Graham
1991-92	H	GMVC	3-0	1664	Hill, Brown 2
	A	GMVC	1-1	890	Butterworth
1992-93	H	GMVC	1-1	1221	Brown
	A	GMVC	1-3	1328	Bancroft
1993-94	H	GMVC	1-2	3120	Price
	A	GMVC	2-1	970	Oxbrow, Clarke
1994-95	H	GMVC	3-2	1713	Taylor, Thomas 2
	A	GMVC	0-1	810	
1995-96	H	GMVC	0-3	851	
	A	GMVC	4-3	952	Pope, Oxbrow, Scott, Alford
1996-97	H	GMVC	0-1	1406	
	A	GMVC	0-1	771	
1997-98	H	GMVC	1-3	1405	Vowden
	A	GMVC	1-1	1041	Pearson

TROWBRIDGE

Season	V	Comp	F-A	Att:	Poppies Scorers
1981-82	H	APL	4-0	1300	Murphy 3, Atkins
	A	APL	1-0	547	Hofbauer
1982-83	H	APL	1-1	916	Goode
	A	APL	1-2	1043	Duggan
1983-84	H	APL	3-2	824	Murphy 2, Hofbauer
	A	APL	2-1	573	Banton, Hofbauer

WEALDSTONE

Season	V	Comp	F-A	Att:	Poppies Scorers
1979-80	H	APL	2-0	2439	Clayton 2
	A	APL	2-2	1970	Evans, Ashby
1980-81	H	APL	0-1	2025	
	A	APL	1-1	837	Guy
1982-83	H	APL	1-3	1020	Murphy
	A	APL	0-4	610	
1983-84	H	APL	1-2	1031	Hofbauer
	A	APL	2-4	781	Palmer, Denyer
1984-85	H	GOLA	0-1	1233	
	A	GOLA	0-1	760	
1985-86	H	GOLA	2-1	1047	Fee, Smith
	A	GOLA	1-3	653	Kabia
1986-87	H	GMVC	0-2	1032	
	A	GMVC	1-2	621	Keast
1987-88	H	GMVC	3-2	1217	Murphy, Tillson, Daley
	A	GMVC	2-0	651	Heywood, Keast

WELLING UNITED

Season	V	Comp	F-A	Att:	Poppies Scorers
1986-87	H	GMVC	5-1	821	Smith, Jeffrey 2, Cavener 2
	A	GMVC	3-0	540	Wharton, Cavener, Jeffrey
1987-88	H	GMVC	1-0	920	Richardson
	A	GMVC	1-3	1059	Smith
1988-89	H	GMVC	2-1	4450	Fuccillo 2
	A	GMVC	1-2	625	Edwards
1989-90	H	GMVC	0-1	1540	
	A	GMVC	0-3	1157	
1990-91	H	GMVC	0-0	2346	
	A	GMVC	0-0	1430	
	H	BLT2	1-0	1145	Emson
1991-92	H	GMVC	1-1	1962	Emson
	A	GMVC	3-2	636	Graham, Gavin, own goal
1992-93	H	GMVC	2-4	1488	Brown, Riley
	A	GMVC	1-1	838	Wright
1993-94	H	GMVC	2-2	1811	Graham, Donald
	A	GMVC	0-2	924	
	H	BLT1/1	0-0	971	
	A	BLT1/2	1-2	457	Thorpe
1994-95	H	GMVC	4-3	1328	Taylor, Alford, Arnold, Stringfellow

178

	A	GMVC	1-2	860	Brown
1995-96	H	GMVC	1-3	1232	Scott
	A	GMVC	0-1	603	
1996-97	H	GMVC	2-3	1420	Stock, Harmon
	A	GMVC	2-1	854	Norman, Mustafa
1997-98	H	GMVC	0-1	1144	
	A	GMVC	2-2	637	Vowden, Norman

WEYMOUTH

Season	V	Comp	F-A	Att:	Poppies Scorers
1979-80	H	APL	3-1	2002	Clayton, Easthall, Ashby
	A	APL	1-3	1027	McIlroy
	H	ALC3	3-1	1463	Ashby, Suddards, Clayton
1980-81	H	APL	1-0	1743	Duggan
	A	APL	2-1	1181	Clarke, Evans
1981-82	H	APL	1-2	1034	Shelton
	A	APL	3-2	781	Atkins, Haverson, Hofbauer
1982-83	H	APL	1-1	954	Evans
	A	APL	1-4	760	Banton
1983-84	H	APL	0-2	1153	
	A	APL	1-1	609	Keast
1984-85	H	GOLA	1-1	1146	Jenas
	A	GOLA	0-3	909	
1985-86	H	GOLA	0-2	999	
	A	GOLA	0-1	720	
1986-87	H	GMVC	3-0	1021	Wood, Cavener, Kellock
	A	GMVC	0-2	923	
1987-88	H	GMVC	3-0	1010	Smith, Edwards, Keast
	A	GMVC	1-2	1940	Crawley
1988-89	H	GMVC	1-0	1231	Keast
	A	GMVC	0-3	802	

WITTON ALBION

Season	V	Comp	F-A	Att:	Poppies Scorers
1991-92	H	GMVC	1-1	1508	Walker
	A	GMVC	0-1	887	
1992-93	H	GMVC	2-1	1090	Donald, Hodges
	A	GMVC	2-4	986	Murphy 2
1993-94	H	GMVC	1-0	1680	Thorpe
	A	GMVC	1-0	789	Graham

WOKING

Season	V	Comp	F-A	Att:	Poppies Scorers
1990-91	H	FAT1	2-0	4421	Graham 2
1992-93	H	GMVC	0-1	1760	
	A	GMVC	2-3	1586	Roderick, Harris
1993-94	H	GMVC	3-0	2054	Martin, Graham, Brown
	A	GMVC	0-0	3130	
1994-95	H	GMVC	0-1	2340	
	A	GMVC	1-3	2277	Thomas
	H	BLTQF	2-1	964	Arnold, Alford
1995-96	H	GMVC	3-0	1671	Alford 2, Oxbrow
	A	GMVC	1-1	2637	Alford
1996-97	H	GMVC	0-0	1912	
	A	GMVC	1-2	2968	Nugent
1997-98	H	GMVC	0-1	1215	
	A	GMVC	1-0	3101	Pearson
	A	SCC2	0-4	559	

WORCESTER CITY

Season	V	Comp	F-A	Att:	Poppies Scorers
1979-80	H	APL	0-0	2706	
	A	APL	4-1	1984	Phipps 2, McIlroy 2
1980-81	H	APL	1-0	1798	Atkins
	A	APL	1-2	2087	Curtis
1981-82	H	APL	0-1	1223	
	A	APL	1-1	1096	Evans
1982-83	H	APL	4-1	784	Banton 2, Hofbauer, Duggan
	A	APL	2-6	884	Duggan, McGoldrick
1983-84	H	APL	0-1	1033	
	A	APL	3-0	861	Denyer, Hofbauer 2
1984-85	H	GOLA	1-0	1167	Jeffrey
	A	GOLA	2-1	1307	Smith, Fee

WYCOMBE WANDERERS

Season	V	Comp	F-A	Att:	Poppies Scorers
1985-86	H	GOLA	4-1	662	Crawley 2, Thacker, Jeffrey
	A	GOLA	0-0	715	
	H	FAT4	2-1	2312	Smith, own goal
1987-88	H	GMVC	3-0	1462	Murphy 2, Smith

	A	GMVC	3-0	1387	Kellock, Crawley 2
1988-89	H	GMVC	2-1	1532	Fuccillo, own goal
	A	GMVC	1-0	4890	Griffith
1989-90	H	GMVC	1-0	2405	Cooke
	A	GMVC	2-2	1996	Slack, Collins
1990-91	H	GMVC	0-1	3020	
	A	GMVC	1-5	4146	Huxford
	H	BLT1	1-0	1435	Moss
1991-92	H	GMVC	1-1	3500	Gavin
	A	GMVC	0-1	4069	
	H	FAC1	1-1	3317	Christie
	A	FAC1R	2-0	5299	Graham, Brown
1992-93	H	GMVC	0-4	3021	
	A	GMVC	2-1	4430	Brown, Hodges

YEOVIL TOWN

Season	V	Comp	F-A	Att:	Poppies Scorers
1979-80	H	APL	5-3	1523	Phipps 2, Jones 2, Evans
	A	APL	1-1	1860	Clayton
1980-81	H	APL	4-0	1671	Evans 2, Martin, Hofbauer
	A	APL	2-1	1269	Forster, own goal
	A	ALC2/1	1-0	1073	Evans
	H	ALC2/2	0-0	1422	
1981-82	H	APL	1-1	1085	Own goal
	A	APL	1-1	1350	Hofbauer
1982-83	H	APL	5-2	1052	Hofbauer 3, Duggan, own goal
	A	APL	1-2	1090	Evans
1983-84	H	APL	2-3	843	Hofbauer, Sandercock
	A	APL	0-2	968	
1984-85	H	GOLA	3-0	891	Shrieves, Smith 2
	A	GOLA	1-1	1375	Jeffrey
1986-87	H	FAT1	2-3	927	Jeffrey, Kabia
1988-89	H	GMVC	1-0	3024	Richardson
	A	GMVC	2-2	2830	Cooke, Edwards
1989-90	H	GMVC	1-0	3608	Collins
	A	GMVC	2-0	1930	Keast, Cooke
1990-91	H	GMVC	1-1	1551	Bancroft
	A	GMVC	1-0	3162	Hunt
1991-92	H	GMVC	2-0	1257	Hill, Graham
	A	GMVC	1-0	1929	Graham
1992-93	H	GMVC	3-0	1337	Hope, Brown 2
	A	GMVC	1-2	2006	Gavin
1993-94	H	GMVC	1-0	1949	Reed
	A	GMVC	0-1	2383	

1994-95	H	GMVC	3-2	1155	Alford 2, Arnold
	A	GMVC	1-1	1938	Clarke
1997-98	H	GMVC	1-1	1116	Pearson
	A	GMVC	0-2	2529	

FA CUP

Season	V	Rd	Opponents	F-A	Att:	Poppies Scorers
1979-80	A	1	Reading	2-4	5877	Phipps 2
1980-81	H	4Q	Banbury Utd	3-0	2114	Evans 2, Hofbauer
	H	1	Maidstone Utd	1-1	2880	Guy
	A	1R	Maidstone Utd	0-0	3156	
	A	12R	Maidstone Utd	1-3	3098	Middleton
1981-82	H	4Q	Kings Lynn	2-1	1972	Evans, Duggan
	A	1	Boston Utd	1-0	2826	Atkins
	H	2	Blackpool	0-3	4439	
1982-83	H	4Q	A P Leamington	3-1	1437	Murphy, Banton 2
	A	1	Walsall	0-3	3471	
1983-84	H	4Q	Sutton Coldfield	3-2	1180	Banton, Needham, Hofbauer
	H	1	Swindon Town	0-7	2880	
1984-85	H	4Q	Harrow Borough	1-1	1416	Jeffrey
	A	4QR	Harrow Borough	2-0	970	Jeffrey, Fee
	H	1	Bournemouth	0-0	2867	
	A	1R	Bournemouth	2-3	3288	Jeffrey, Alexander
1985-86	A	4Q	Chelmsford City	0-1	1319	
1986-87	H	1Q	Lowestoft Town	2-1	832	Jeffrey, Crawley
	A	2Q	Tiptree Utd	3-0	345	Crawley, Jeffrey, Genovese
	H	3Q	Corby Town	2-0	1545	Richardson, Genovese
	H	4Q	Windsor & Eton	1-0	1024	Kellock
	H	1	Gillingham	0-3	2845	
1987-88	A	1Q	Wisbech Town	0-2	740	
1988-89	A	1Q	Ware	3-0	510	Cooke 2, Green
	A	2Q	Gt Yarmouth	3-0	510	Fuccillo, Wright, Keast
	H	3Q	Boreham Wood	4-0	1549	Moss, Cooke 2, Edwards
	A	4Q	Wycombe W	2-1	2454	Cooke 2
	H	1	Dartford	2-1	3024	Lewis, Griffith
	H	2	Bristol Rovers	2-1	4450	Cooke 2
	H	3	Halifax Town	1-1	5800	Griffith
	A	3R	Halifax Town	3-2	5632	Lewis, Cooke 2
	A	4	Charlton Athletic	1-2	16001	Cooke
1989-90	H	1	Northampton Tn	0-1	6100	
1990-91	A	4Q	Chelmsford City	0-0	2265	
	H	4QR	Chelmsford City	1-2	3292	Brown
1991-92	A	1Q	Wisbech Town	3-0	1017	Brown 2, Christie
	H	2Q	Braintree	3-1	1609	Graham, Jones, Hill

	H	3Q	Heybridge Swifts	3-0	1587	Graham, Brown, own goal
	H	4Q	Stafford Rangers	0-0	1785	
	A	4QR	Stafford Rangers	2-0	1070	Christie, Jones
	H	1	Wycombe W	1-1	3317	Christie
	A	1R	Wycombe W	2-0	5299	Graham, Brown
	H	2	Maidstone Utd	2-1	2750	Brown, own goal (Oxbrow)
	A	3	Blackburn Rovers	1-4	13321	Brown
1992-93	H	4Q	Corby Town	2-1	3273	Brown, Murphy
	A	1	Gillingham	2-3	3962	Brown, Hill
1993-94	H	4Q	Canvey Island	3-1	2191	Thorpe, Wright 2
	A	1	Kidderminster H	0-3	3775	
1994-95	A	4Q	Solihull Borough	4-2	1181	Brown, Thomas 2, Alfc
	H	1	Plymouth Argyle	0-1	4602	
1995-96	H	4Q	Bromsgrove R	0-0	2427	
	A	4QR	Bromsgrove R	2-2	1426	Scott, Alford
	H	4Q2R	Bromsgrove R	1-2	2283	Alford
1996-97	A	1Q	Rocester	3-0	423	Pope, Mustafa, Lynch
	H	2Q	Atherstone Utd	0-0	1228	
	A	2QR	Atherstone Utd	6-1	682	Nyamah, Norman, Carter 2, May 2
	H	3Q	Bedworth Utd	0-1	1461	
1997-98	H	1Q	Mirrlees Blackstone	0-1	768	Nuttell
	H	2Q	Cambridge City	1-1	921	Berry
	A	2QR	Cambridge City	4-2	498	Berry, Adams, Ridgwa Wilkes
	H	3Q	Hinckley United	0-1	1002	

FA TROPHY

Season	V	Rd	Opponents	F-A	Att:	Poppies Scorers
1979-80	A	1	Merthyr Tydfil	0-3	1756	
1980-81	A	1	Gravesend/N'fleet	3-2	1024	Evans 2, own goal
	H	2	Mossley	0-1	2427	
1981-82	H	1	Mossley	0-1	1286	
1982-83	H	3Q	Barking	2-2	909	Hofbauer, Banton
	A	3QR	Barking	0-0	**	
	A	32R	Barking	2-0	**	Duggan, Chamberlain
	A	1	Dulwich Hamlet	2-4	607	Goode, Duggan
1983-84	A	3Q	Dulwich Hamlet	3-4	275	Hofbauer, Palmer, Kirk
1984-85	A	3Q	Macclesfield Town	2-0	664	Alexander, Smith
	A	1	Burton Albion	1-2	1286	Shrieves
1985-86	A	1	Sutton United	1-0	773	Shrieves
	A	2	Slough Town	2-1	871	Fee, Smith
	A	3	Worthing	0-0	602	
	A	3R	Worthing	2-1	1365	Smith, Jeffrey
	H	4	Wycombe W	2-1	2312	Smith, own goal
	A	SF1	Runcorn	0-0	2023	
	H	SF2	Runcorn	0-2	4032	
1986-87	H	1	Yeovil Town	2-3	927	Jeffrey, Kabia
1987-88	A	1	Aylesbury United	1-1	1222	Smith
	H	1R	Aylesbury United	5-1	1239	Richardson 2, Murphy 3
	A	2	Altrincham	1-1	881	Richardson
	H	2R	Altrincham	2-3	1021	Keast, Smith
1988-89	A	1	Basingstoke	1-1	1200	Moss
	H	1 R	Basingstoke	5-3	2306	Beech, Wright, Moss, Griffiths, Edwards
	A	2	Gravesend/N'fleet	1-1	1119	Beech
	H	2R	Gravesend/N'fleet	1-2	2801	Moss
1989-90	H	1	Wokingham	0-2	2376	
1990-91	H	1	Woking	2-0	4421	Graham 2
	A	2	Barrow	0-0	3033	
	H	2R	Barrow	2-1	2522	Slack, Quow
	A	3	Emley	2-3	2726	Walwyn
1991-92	A	1	V S Rugby	1-0	1790	Hill
	A	2	Bashley	3-2	1065	Culpin, Hill, Brown
	A	3	Marine	1-2	1111	Keast
1992-93	H	1	Bromsgrove R	0-0	1723	
	A	1R	Bromsgrove R	1-4	1269	Riley
1993-94	H	1	Stevenage Boro'	2-1	2414	Wright, Reed
	H	2	Billingham Synth	2-2	2076	Donald, Graham

185

	A	2R	Billingham Synth	1-3	842	Stringfellow
1994-95	A	1	Walton & Hersham	2-2	398	Holden, Howe
	H	1R	Walton & Hersham	1-0	1478	Stringfellow
	A	2	Boreham Wood	1-2	800	Stringfellow
1995-96	H	1	St Albans City	1-1	1577	Pope
	A	1R	St Albans City	3-2	785	Ibrahim, Alford, Pope
	A	2	Slough Town	2-1	1058	Scott, Gynn
	A	3	Stevenage Boro'	0-3	2219	
1996-97	H	1	Chelmsford City	0-1	1528	
1997-98	H	1	Dorchester	1-0	1341	Mutchell
	A	2	Northwich Victoria	0-4	1225	

** Official attendances not recorded due to administration error.

186

FA TROPHY

FINALISTS FROM 1979/80 TO 1997/98

1980	Dagenham	2	Mossley	1
1981	Bishop Stortford	1	Sutton United	0
1982	Enfield	1	Altrincham	0
1983	Telford United	2	Northwich Victoria	1
1984*	Northwich Victoria	2(1)	Bangor City	1(1)
1985	Wealdstone	2	Boston United	1
1986	Altrincham	1	Runcorn	0
1987*	Kidderminster Harriers	2(0)	Burton Albion	1(0)
1988*	Enfield	3(0)	Telford United	2(0)
1989	Telford United	1	Macclesfield Town	0
1990	Barrow	3	Leek Town	0
1991	Wycombe Wanderers	2	Kidderminster Harriers	1
1992	Colchester United	3	Witton Albion	1
1993	Wycombe Wanderers	4	Runcorn	1
1994	Woking	2	Runcorn	1
1995	Woking	2	Kidderminster Harriers	1
1996	Macclesfield Town	3	Northwich Victoria	1
1997	Woking	1	Dagenham & Redbridge	0
1998	Cheltenham Town	1	Southport	0

* After a replay.

LEAGUE CUP

Season	V	Rd	Opponents	F-A	Att:	Poppies Scorers
1979-80*	A	2	AP Leamington	4-0	733	Hughes, Clayton, Phipps, Phillips
	H	3	Weymouth	3-1	1463	Ashby, Suddards, Clayton
	H	SF1	Northwich Vic	0-0	1643	
	A	SF2	Northwich Vic	1-3	1395	Evans
1980-81*	A	2/1	Yeovil Town	1-0	1073	Evans
	H	2/2	Yeovil Town	0-0	1422	
	H	3	Barnet	1-1	1331	Atkins
	A	3R	Barnet	4-1	1337	Evans, Suddards, Atkins, Phipps
	A	SF1	Barrow	2-0	1013	Duggan, Phipps
	H	SF2	Barrow	5-1	1245	Evans 2, Atkins, Clarke, Phipps
	A	FI	Altrincham	0-2	1887	
	H	F2	Altrincham	2-1	2095	Atkins, Guy
1981-82*	A	2/1	Northwich Vic	3-3	758	Atkins, Murphy, Evans
	H	2/2	Northwich Vic	0-2	1276	
1982-83*	A	1/1	Bangor City	1-6	720	Goode
	H	1/2	Bangor City	1-1	556	Murphy
1983-84+	H	1/1	Nuneaton Boro'	4-2	1068	Murphy 2, Bradd, Hofbauer
	A	1/2	Nuneaton Boro'	1-1	885	Hofbauer
	A	2/1	Runcorn	0-4	656	
	H	2/2	Runcorn	1-1	545	Shelton
1984-85+	A	1/1	Boston United	4-0	1004	Keast, Fee, Dawson
	H.	1/2	Boston United	3-2	902	Jeffrey, Jenas, Sellers
	H	2/1	Northwich Vic	1-0	657	Shrieves
	A	2/2	Northwich Vic	2-1	769	Shrieves, Alexander
	H	3	Altrincham	1-2	1102	Shrieves
1985-86+	H	1/1	Cheltenham Tn	0-1	920	
	A	1/2	Cheltenham Tn	1-5	1293	Crawley
1986-87+*	H	1	Telford United	0-0	728	
	A	1R	Telford United	2-0	851	Lewis, Keast
	H	2	Boston United	3-2	437	Keast, Jeffrey 2
	A	3	Altrincham	2-2	602	Smith, Crawley
	H	3R	Altrincham	2-0	750	Smith, Crawley
	A	4	Runcorn	2-1	617	Cavener, Smith
	A	SF	Aylesbury Utd	2-0	746	Heywood, Daley
	H	F	Hendon	3-1	1809	Kellock, Keast, Smith
1987-88+*	H	1	VS Rugby	1-0	662	Smith
	A	2	Stafford Rangers	1-0	1185	Murphy

188

	H	3	Northwich Victoria	2-3	661	Ward, Murphy
1988-89++	A	1	Worksop	3-0	356	Fuccillo, Keast, Wright
	A	2	Leytonstone	0-3	206	
1989-90+	A	2	Barnet	2-3	786	Genovese, Graham
1990-91+	H	1	Wycombe W	1-0	1435	Moss
	H	2	Welling Utd	1-0	1145	Emson
	H	SF1	Sutton Utd	0-2	1104	
	A	SF2	Sutton Utd	1-4	707	Graham
1991-92+	A	1	Colchester Utd	0-4	1298	
1992-93**	A	1	Kidderminster	0-3	624	
1993-94+	H	1/1	Welling Utd	0-0	971	
	A	1/2	Welling Utd	1-2	457	Thorpe
1994-95 +	A	2	Kidderminster	5-1	914	Brown 2, Stringfellow, Magee
	H	QF	Woking	2-1	964	Arnold, Alford
	H	SF1	Dag & Redbridge	0-2	1033	
	A	SF2	Dag & Redbridge	4-2	750	Arnold 2, Brown, Thomas
	A	F1	Bromsgrove R	1-4	1393	Clarke
	H	F2	Bromsgrove R	1-6	1311	Alford
1995-96*+	H	2	Stevenage Boro'	2-1	808	Stringfellow, Harmon
	H	QF	Slough Town	2-0	646	Pope, Harmon
	A	SF1	Bromsgrove R	0-2	650	
	H	SF2	Bromsgrove R	2-1	773	Gynn, Mustafa
1996-97 *+	H	1	Slough Town	1-0	702	May
	H	2	Farnborough Town	0-2	503	
1997-98*+	A	1	Dover Athletic	3-1	520	Wilkes, Costello, Norman
	A	2	Woking	0-4	559	

*	APLC	Alliance Premier League Cup
+	BLT	Bob Lord Trophy
+*	GMVCC	General Motors Acceptance Corporation Cup
++	CLBCC	Club Call Cup
	BLTDW	Bob Lord Drink Wise Trophy
*+	SCC	Spalding Challenge Cup

LEAGUE CUP
PREVIOUS FINALISTS

Season	Winners	Runners - up
1979-80	Northwich Victoria	Altrincham
1980-81	Altrincham	*Kettering Town*
1981-82	Weymouth	Enfield
1982-83	Runcorn	Scarborough
1983-84	Scarborough	Barnet
1984-85	Runcorn	Maidstone United
1985-86	Stafford Rangers	Barnet
1986-87	*Kettering Town*	Hendon
1987-88	Horwich RMI	Weymouth
1988-89	Barnet	Hyde United
1989-90	Yeovil Town	Kidderminster Harriers
1990-91	Sutton United	Barrow
1991-92	Wycombe W	Runcorn
1992-93	Northwich Victoria	Wycombe Wanderers
1993-94	Macclesfield Town	Yeovil Town
1994-95	Bromsgrove R	*Kettering Town*
1995-96	Bromsgrove R	Macclesfield Town
1996-97	Kidderminster H	Macclesfield Town
1997-98	Morecambe	Woking

BIBLIOGRAPHY

Non-League Football Fact Book - Tony Williams.
Rothmans Football Yearbooks 1988 - 1996 - Jack Rollin.
The 1995-96, 96-97 - Official PFA Footballballers *Factfile* - Barry J
Hugman.
The Northamptonshire Evening Telegraph - from 1979.
The Foxes Alaphabet - Paul Taylor and Dave Smith.
Numerous Kettering Town FC home and away programmes.